JUNGLE ODYSSEY

A Soldier's Memoirs

Major General **Ashok Kalyan Verma**, AVSM (Retd)

KW Publishers Pvt Ltd
New Delhi

First reprint October 2013

KNOWLEDGE WORLD

KW Publishers Pvt Ltd
4676/21, First Floor, Ansari Road, Daryaganj, New Delhi 110002
Email: knowledgeworld@vsnl.net Tel.: +91.11.23263498/43528107

www.kwpub.com

All rights reserved. No part of this book may be reproduced or transmitted in any form or by any means, electronic or mechanical, including photocopying, recording or by any information storage and retrieval system, without permission in writing.

ISBN 978-93-81904-75-6

© 2013, Ashok Kalyan Verma

Photo Credits – Cover & Back Cover Photo – Teesta Verma

*Dedicated
to my Beloved Wife and
companion – "Usha"
and to the memory of
"Ammaji"
My Great Grandmother*

Contents

1.	Introduction	1
2.	Jungle Odyssey	3
3.	The Tiger's Tail	6
4.	The Alipore Zoo Tigress	14
5.	Introducing 'Deva–Pitta' and His Shikar Episodes	16
6.	Jabalpur — Kashmir and Nagpur	26
7.	Nagpur — The Jhilpa Man-Eater Leopard	33
8.	Mandla — 1946	51
9.	The Leopard Across the Narbada	57
10.	The Timni Tiger	61
11.	School At Nainital	70
12.	Hyderabad — Police Action 1948	74
13.	Nanded — Kaulash — 1949-50	80
14.	State Capital — Hyderabad	89
15.	Nainital — 1947-52	92

Joining The Army

16.	Dehradun — The National Defence Academy	100
17.	The Military Wing	106
18.	The Asarori Tiger	110
19.	Commissioning	115
20.	Fatehgarh — The Regimental Centre	118
21.	Joining The Battalion	120

Some More Shikar Episodes

22.	Kinwat	129
23.	The Shimla Hills — Sabathu	145
24.	Romance and Marriage	148
25.	'Matchless' Trip	153
26.	Marriage And After	156
27.	Train To The North-East	159
28.	Lohit Frontier Division	164
29.	Walong	168
30.	The Limhaipur Tigers	172
31.	Elephants	179
32.	The Second Encounter	189
33.	The Nilgiri Bison Or Gaur	191
34.	Just Plain Soldiering	195
35.	The Tso-Kar Snow-Leopard	202
36.	Tiger in The Triangle	208
37.	Epilogue	212
38.	Some Thoughts	213
39.	About the Author	219

ACKNOWLEDGEMENTS

Many friends have helped and guided me in the task. Prominent are Karen McKay (Lt Col, US Army, Retd), Col Kul Bhushan Deswal, Lt Gen T P Singh.

Within the family, Teesta, Dhruv and Vidur, Kunal and Dipti for use of their wildlife and other photographs.

Mr Harkesh Dagar, our very kind and helpful neighbour in handling the computer. Mr Vijay Deswal, Commandant 2nd Battalion ITBP at Bandrol, Kullu for assistance provided by him and his staff.

Lt Gen Sushil Pillai of the Assam Regiment for his useful tips and meaningful suggestions. Sushil had shared one of the episodes with us as narrated in the Second Encounter with the Elephants.

INTRODUCTION

Jim Corbett's wonderful books on the hunting of big game in India, began to appear after the conclusion of the Second World War and in the period just before India gained her Independence. This great hunter and lover of wildlife, set a pace for others which could not be easily matched either in the beauty and simplicity of descriptive writing, truth of the story, or in the hair-raising thrill of adventure.

Apart from the simplicity of Jim Corbett's writings, were his identifying closely with the people of Kumaon with a touch of abiding affection for the poor of "his India". He was an Englishman of an extra-ordinary kind who left his mark in the country even after leaving it in 1948. It is no wonder that the Corbett Wildlife National Park, which nestles in the proximity of his beloved village of Kaladhungi, preserves as an abiding memorial for this very good and simple human being.

Even today, almost seventy years after Jim Corbett's books first appeared, he remains a well read and popular author world-wide.

The ambiance of "Shikar" which prevailed in the central Indian region of 'CP'(Central Province – now Madhya Pradesh) owing to the abundant wildlife and jungles of the area, was 'heady' stuff for us growing boys. Civil servants of those days were encouraged to keep in touch of the rural areas by being "shikaris". Early exposure to some events and encounters cast a spell on us during those growing years. Being sent off to School in " Jim Corbett's Nainital" in July 1947 further added a lifelong addiction to the Sport of big-game hunting.

My purpose in writing these stories in "Jungle Odyssey"- 'A Soldier's Memoirs', is to preserve the memory of a by-gone era. 'Shikar' or the hunting and killing of wildlife as a sport has not only disappeared but even such books on Shikar are frowned upon as some kind of evil that has denuded the Indian jungles of wildlife. It is with some hesitation and trepidation that I have undertaken this effort.

I maintain that organized and properly regulated 'Shikar' was not the cause of such alarming destruction of wildlife in India. Instead, I believe the breakdown of lower level governance and any kind of discipline has seen the growth of corruption in almost all walks of life. Being the son of a civil servant of the earlier era, I have seen the change and total lack of commitment and disinterest in district level functionaries since those earlier times. The greed for making money hand over fist seems to be the culture that prevails.

The Army was a much respected and sought after profession. It was a way of life, with its own value system. However, I found it very disturbing during my service to find that 'Shikar' was a very loosely applied term to the blatant misuse of vehicles and weapons in the wanton killing of wildlife. Perhaps it was too late that I got drawn into an effort to turn into a 'conservationist'.

Jungle lore and the knowledge of birds and animals however actually served in the sharpening of your sensitivity to the living world around you, so essential for the infantry officer.

April 2013   **Ashok Kalyan Verma**

JUNGLE ODYSSEY

From a bush with thorns Comes the beautiful rose
From a broken heart Comes Powerful prose
From a cramped cocoon Comes a butterfly new
From a tough mountain climb
Comes a breathtaking view

—Maria Fontane

These are some mixed stories, Shikar memories and the jungle memoirs of a soldier.

After witnessing the wanton destruction of wildlife and forests, during the last half century or so country wide, it is with some hesitation that I write this book. 'Shikar' has become an unspoken of thing of the past.

The events narrated took place in an era that has gone by . Things can never be the same again.

A blanket ban on Shikar has hardly helped and denied the genuine sportsman's monitoring and selective interaction with wildlife. The poacher and complete lawlessness holds sway.

I am attempting a potpourri of shikar memories and a sort of nostalgic memoir of happy days of my childhood and those spent in the Army. Shikar or big game hunting in the Indian jungles, ideally prepared the infantry officer, which I chose to be, for the sharpness of perception and quick responses needed in his profession. Knowledge of birds and animals, and interest in all living beings, added a unique flavour to soldiering.

These wildlife related episodes and stories cover events of over 70 past years or so. Most of these occurred in the districts of central India, which then formed a part of Central Province (CP).

It was in 1939, as a four-year-old, that I, along with other sibling, had for the first time seen a tiger stalking a herd of Chital and Barasingha, browsing in a sunlit glade in the late afternoon in the wildlife sanctuary of Kanha. This sighting of a tiger as a four-year-old, is the distinct event related to wildlife that must act as the start point of these jungle memories.

My father was at that time posted at. Jabalpur – from where we had driven in the newly acquired family car to Kanha-Kisli Sanctuary. My father was a junior Provincial Civil Servant then and was posted between 1939 and 1947 in Jabalpur and thereafter, from time to time in some of the adjoining districts. Father was later also posted in between in the then Provincial capital of the Central Province at Nagpur from mid 1942 to end of 1945.

Many of the districts of CP had plenty of jungle cover and were well known for shikar. In keeping with the prevalent culture during the time, Father had developed a great fondness for the sport. As growing boys, it was exciting sharing some of my father's shikar adventures as we grew up. Being the elder of the two brothers by a couple of years, I had the advantage being often with him.

Civil Servants during the colonial period were officially encouraged to indulge in casual shikar. Father was later posted as the Additional District Magistrate at Mandla. The Kanha Sanctuary was located within this district The district town of Mandla was located on the Narmada River, about 100 kilometres south of Jabalpur. Kanha-Kisli was further south across the Narmada River.

Kanha in central India is located in the eastern segment of the Satpura in the Mekhal Range which forms the watershed between the Narmada and Mahanadi. Narmada River flows westwards past

Mandla and then Jabalpur, towards the Arabian Sea whilst the Mahanadi drains into the Bay of Bengal towards the southeast through Orissa.

Later in July 1947, a month before India became Independent, we brothers were sent off to school in Nainital. Well known Indian business family of the Birlas had set up a new school – Birla Vidya Mandir, in the existing hilltop estate which had earlier housed successive schools since 1877. The hilltop school campus was surrounded with a fairly dense oak forest. Located on top of the eastern ridge, beneath the Sher-ka-Danda peak, it overlooked the Nainital lake and the upper township of Malital. It was at an imposing height of about 7800 feet above sea level.

Nainital to us brothers was doubly exciting, as even then as 12 and 10 year old boys we had both been introduced to the book- *'Maneaters of kumaon'* under our father's guidance. Jim Corbett, the author and re-known shikari, was already a hero figure in our eyes. His narrative form of story telling and his great love for the people of Kumaon appealed immensely to us. The backdrop of being in the same mountain environment was thrilling. We had joined school at Nainital in July 1947, when we learnt later that he had sold his farm and place at Kaladungi and had migrated to Kenya.

In the CP districts our schooling had been quite disturbed owing to Father's frequent moves and we having had several bouts of malaria. The shift to Nainital was to overcome these shortcomings . Smaller district towns had indifferent schooling and malaria was rampant.

These jungle memories are of a happy, carefree childhood, spending time with our Father, imbibing the beauty of the jungle. The country was far less crowded those days, with the population roughly one third of what it is today. We were greatly drawn to learning about birds and wild life as a natural part of our exposure. I confess that we found routine schooling dull and unappealing.

THE TIGER'S TAIL

As an introduction to these jungle stories, I would like to narrate an incident that occurred in March 1965.

I had joined the Army in 1952 and was commissioned as an officer in June 1956. Having done six years thereafter in a hardship posting in remote corners of North East Frontier Agency (NEFA), I was posted in July 1962 to Dehradun to the Indian Military Academy. It was a prized posting where my wife and children could join me.

The unexpected events of 1962 in the autumn in which my own unit, 2nd Battalion of the Rajput Regiment, was almost wiped out in the Chinese attack on 20 October on the Nam Ka Chu, cast a painful shadow . It seemed providential that I had moved out of my Battalion just in time before the disastrous events of autumn of 1962. Losing most of my comrades and companions in that brutal war so soon after my leaving them came as a painful blow.

After two years at the Academy I qualified for and was nominated to attend the truncated seven-months Defence Services Staff College at Wellington in the beautiful Nilgiris in Tamil Nadu. At the end of the Staff College course, I was posted to a new raising of my Regiment – taking place at Fatehgarh (The Rajput Regimental Centre, is located in central UP). I was granted a months joining time and leave before reporting at Fatehgarh.

After a brief stop over at Chennai (Madras) to collect a Standard Herald car, we as a family drove north by road. This meant journeying along the eastern coast before cutting across to Hyderabad. This trip northwards covered almost the whole length of peninsular India. It gave my family and me a unique opportunity to visit en route many of the places we had spent time in during boyhood years, when my father was serving in these places following the Hyderabad Police Action. We had many years previously spent our winter holidays between 1948 and 1955 with him at Adilabad, Nanded and later Hyderabad, the state capital. Our school at Nainital had a three-and-a- half month annual closure for winter. There was no summer break.

In March 1965 we drove from Hyderabad to Adilabad and passed through to Nagpur next day. We next got to Balaghat, the district at the southern side of the Kanha area. The basic idea was to visit the Kanha-Kisli sanctuary to revive memories of the past. After getting all the permits and permissions for visiting the Sanctuary, we entered the Reserve from the south at Mukki.

*****

Our road journey had gone smoothly. In the almost two decades since we had been there little seemed changed in Hyderabad and the areas we traversed. I was full of shikar tales for the children. Just a few miles short of Adilabad, I pointed out a place where on an evenings jeep drive, we had chanced upon a family of five tigers.

Very near the place where we had sighted the family of tigers was a large water reservoir in the midst of the jungle called Mavala. In those days following the Police Action, the area around the Mavala reservoir and in the district generally, there seemed to be an unusually large number of the big cats. Some one attributed this to the Hyderabadi Razakars before the police action being indiscriminately armed, having largely poached and destroyed most of the deer and nilgai. But wild-boar and carnivores, seemed

to abound. Razakars, being mainly Muslims, did not shoot the pigs which were in large numbers. Carnivorous animals were not usually tackled by the Razakar poachers, and the tigers and panthers seemed to thrive on cattle-lifting from the scattered villages.

All this had changed in the decade and a half since we had been there, and the old caretaker at the Adilabad Dak bungalow told us that rarely did they now hear of any sightings of the big cats. During our overnight stay at the Dak Bungalow, the old caretaker gathered some of the surviving members of supporting staff of my father's days. We sat on the flagstone floor of the verandah, talking of old days and events into the night.

It was sad to learn that David, my fathers driver, had died in an accident some years before. He had accompanied me when I sat up on a leopard kill near a village called Boath many years ago. I had then bagged my first leopard as a 13 year old that evening.

*****

From Mukki we drove on to Kisli, from where we were to get to the Kanha Rest House area located overlooking the beautiful and vast Kanha meadow. As we got closer to our destination area, our expectations were quite aroused. We hoped to be getting to Kanha by afternoon to be able to go out on the evening sighting trip on elephant back. We were entering Kipling's 'Jungle Book' country.

We turned north from Mukki forest barrier and drove along the forest road along the western edge of the Sanctuary. The gravel forest road was as smooth and well maintained as could be. It was mid-march and the Sal forest was at its resplendent best. A kind of peace and quietude seemed to settle over all of us in the car as we sped almost noiselessly along the straight groove of the road through the dense jungle. The Sal jungle remains dark green almost throughout the year, each tree beautiful and majestic. Sal forests tend to occur in pure strands. In February and March the

THE TIGER'S TAIL

leaves are shed, but just as soon renewed, changing hues from brownish red to pale green as they grow. In March-April, the trees suddenly bloom prolifically. The small off-white flowers impart a unique look to the forest and their mild scent fills up the morning and evening air.

The new leaves looking polished and glistened in the afternoon light and the odour of the crushed leaves of the previous years windfall stirred memories of the past. Occasionally a shower of Sal seeds carpeted the floor, the propeller- like winged seeds littering the road with the softer velvet green hue. An occasional Tree Pie flitted across the straight road and then a Racket Tailed Drongo flew across with its two distinct black blobs, trailing its flight. It is called '*Bring-Raj*' in its hindi name, which means the king of the Bumble Bee. This beautiful bird resides in thick Sal and Bamboo jungle. It is a mischievous mimic and Jim Corbett mentions how he once heard this bird give out the alarm call of a chital.

In 1965 the larger Wildlife Project Tiger Reserve had not been formed as it exists today. It was still confined to the old Kanha-Kisli Sanctuary. We entered the main Sanctuary at the Kishli Forest Barrier and drove eastward towards Kanha's heart centre. The low slung Standard Herald car softly purring along on the gravel forest road. With a widening ravine on the left, the road climbed smoothly up some rising ground. I was a bit keyed up with some vague expectation and was grumbling to myself at not coming across any wildlife in the few kilometers we had covered. Usha and the children, too, seemed gripped with some silent expectation. We were all eyes and ears looking around as we drove on.

The road curved around, topping the last of the rising ground and the car took the gentle turn to almost run slap into a large tiger sitting in the middle of the road, in a patch of afternoon sunlight. Who was more surprised at the sudden meeting! We in the car or the tiger? Both of us seemed equally startled at the sudden

closeness. As I stopped the car almost in a reflex action, the tiger hurriedly moved towards the side of the road and stood barely ten to fifteen paces away from me, looking somewhat down at me in the driver's seat. His facial expression, however, was more of curiosity and he fixed his yellow eyes looking down at me. Every detail on his magnificent face and head visible from such close quarters, his mouth slightly ajar showing the tip of his pink tongue.

He was the most massive tiger I had ever seen, his face with the prominent round fringe of a big male. Time stood still for some minutes, as we remained frozen with awe at the sudden confrontation. It would be extremely dangerous if the powerful animal lost his temper for being hustled so suddenly. We in the

Kunal and Teesta, 1965

car remained spell bound and nobody moved or uttered a sound. I was acutely aware of the grave danger we faced but just held my breath, admiring the magnificent tiger from such close proximity. With the round face of a fully mature male, every detail of his was so clearly visible.

For a very long minute, there was no change in the tiger's curious expression while staring us down. Then very slowly he turned to get past the car. He stiffened his legs awkwardly and unhurriedly started drifting away with his tail raised vertically like a tom-cat. He slowly began to move away into the jungle unhurriedly.

I waited deliberately for a few minutes to let him get away before driving on. I found that unconsciously I had been holding my breath. It was a close encounter and could have led to an accident. As we drove on further the full realization of the dangerous possibilities hit me. My whole family had shared the breathtaking encounter with me.

We were lucky to have gotten away as we did. Later, that same evening we did see another tiger during the elephant ride. This was from a considerable distance and in the fading light as dusk was setting in. This second tiger looked sleeker and was probably a tigress.

* * * * *

A Post script here: Many years later, in mid 90's, well after I had retired from the Army, I accompanied my daughter Teesta to the Kanha Tiger Reserve.

By this time several well run resorts had sprung up at Kisli and further south at Mukki. The expanded Project Tiger Reserve included several villages that had been relocated elsewhere. The jungle had quickly reclaimed most of the area.

In keeping with the expectation and desire of the large influx

of tourist and visitors, the Park staff had worked out a method that would enable almost everyone to get to see a tiger, from elephant back in an unhurried manner.

Mahouts who were excellent trackers themselves, on elephants would set out everyday in the early hours of the morning and by following fresh pug marks and alarm calls, they 'homed' onto a tiger. With hand-held radio sets the mahouts with the three elephants manage to keep the tiger roughly between them. Keeping a safe distance, yet enabling the visiting tourist to see and photograph the tiger in the natural surroundings without disturbing the animal too much. This method seems to work admirably .The mahouts seem to recognize most of the tigers in the park, and generally respect their individual tolerance level. It was a revelation to see how the tiger seemed to completely ignore the elephants and the camera-wielding tourists. In one case a young tigress got so bored with the proceedings that she rolled over in a sunny patch in the tall grass and went to sleep – exposing her belly and seemingly completely relaxed lying on her back.

On the third day of our stay we got word from the Park radio network that a male tiger had been located by the Kisli Mahouts. It took us some time to get to the place in the Gypsy jeep by the forest roads. We were told that we were the last batch allowed to view this tiger. My daughter Teesta and I got onto a medium size female elephant to get us close enough to the tiger to take some photographs. The tiger was now in the cover of some saplings, the foliage of which did not give us a clear view.

Perhaps the Mahout of our elephant got us too close to the hidden tiger, who was clearly showing signs of irritation. Ours was a medium-sized female elephant which by following a dry nala bed adversely placed us even on elephant back, at the same level as the partially-concealed tiger. We both saw him watching us through the foliage. Teesta photographed the yellow, glaring eyes, and the tiger seemed to hear the camera's shutter sound and

growled in the most menacing manner. A tiger's growl – even a low one has an awesome affect and our Mahout quickly got us out of the exposed nala. The photograph on the cover of this book was the result of this encounter.

Putting the two events together – we had indeed been very lucky that in March 1965 the annoyed Tiger had only raised his tail to convey his anger and had not precipitated a charge. Even a growl then would have shaken us enough. It also shows how sharp the hearing power and eyesight of the great beast is. He had heard the very slight sound of the hand held camera.

I later asked others, including the leading staff members of the Wildlife Institute of India located at Dehradun, what the tigers tail raising conveyed. No clear opinion or view was ever expressed. Domestic cats, particularly tom cats, do raise their tail vertically during courtship display.

THE ALIPORE ZOO TIGRESS

After the successful conclusion of the Bangladesh War, my unit returned to Agartala from Dhaka in March 1972. After some time we were permitted to take leave. I was at Dehradun when I was recalled to Agartala in Tripura to provide evidence in a Court Martial proceedings being held there. It was an unpleasant task, for which I felt a great distaste. The school holidays for the summer months had begun, so I hoped that my bringing my family members with me for a short visit would be given a blind eye by the higher ups. Families were still strictly not allowed in the operational area.

My 11-year-old son Kunal accompanied me by train to Kolkata, from where we were to fly across Bangladesh by the Indian Airlines flight to Agartala. After the war, my men and officers were permitted the use of the airline facilities. My wife and daughter were to follow a few days later.

At Kolkata we had several hours in hand before we had to be at Dum Dum Airport to catch the flight to Agartala. So Kunal and I decided to go around the Alipore Zoo to while away the time. We were watching a tigress restlessly exercising herself within the confined space of the cage. She was briskly moving to and fro, turning restlessly to continue her activity in a fluid and flowing motion. How long she had been doing this we could not guess.

Apart from the two of us, there was a betel-nut chewing young man with a packet of peanuts in his hands, watching the tigress from a safe distance. For some unaccountable reason he was making loud, obscene remarks at the tigress. He would occasionally also pelt the caged animal with the peanuts he was eating and was finding it hilariously funny doing so. I noticed the tigress's expression of annoyance within the cage as she continued her to and fro restless movement.

Something in her annoyed expression made me pull Kunal back as she abruptly turned and squirted a full blast of her urine at the offending young man tormenting her through the bars of her cage. The full blast struck the man on his lower face and chest, drenching his shirt completely. Meanwhile, thereafter the Tigress continued her restless to and fro exercising without a pause

The moral to this story. A tiger, even a caged one has to be treated with respect and dignity....

Tigress marking her territory

INTRODUCING 'DEVA –PITTA' AND HIS SHIKAR EPISODES

The old hunter does not repine; he "looks not mournfully into the Past, it cometh not again;" rather he looks joyously back to days when he lived indeed !

— (Brig Gen R G Burton – TIGERS)

These episodes occurred during the period of more than half a century – an interesting period of great change in India. It gives some idea of my parent's family, but essentially focuses on my father (Deva-Pitta) as the central figure. The episodes narrated have been a part of the family lore that we grew up with. These events occurred in the day to day life of the junior civil servant serving in the districts of 'CP,' as Central Province was then called. 'Shikar' was officially encouraged and treated as an asset with junior civil servants serving in the districts. Generally, central India's Central Province districts were covered with the most varied and extensive forests at that time.

Junior civil servants were encouraged to spend more time in the rural areas being administered, so that they had a better 'feel' for their job. Comfortable tentage was provided for the touring officer's stay, which was staged forward and setup before the 'sahib' arrived. Bullock carts were the main form of transportation, but some times camels and the odd elephant would be provided.

INTRODUCING 'DEVA –PITTA' AND HIS SHIKAR EPISODES

Invariably the village folk would give the visitor the latest news, or shikar *'Khabar'* and this would sometimes lead to some exciting jungle event. Tiger or panther kills in the area were reported as often valuable villagers domestic cattle had been lost to the predator.

In the beginning as a probationer, Father took steps to further his interest in Shikar. With the guidance of his senior colleagues, he acquired a . 405 calibre American magazine rifle, with a 'take down' action, which fired a 300-grain bullet propelled by cordite. This was a heavy, powerful, rugged and reliable weapon. This rifle was quite popular with the big game hunters in India at the time. He also acquired a 32 inch barrel length, double-barrel hammer shotgun made by Johnstons in England. Later, as we grew up, the task of cleaning and oiling the weapons by young brother Vijay and myself was routine. We were also taught the do's and dont's of the handling of weapons.

We were a family of four children, two girls followed by two boys, born between 1932 and 1937. Our mother and the two elder sisters formed the other half of the family, whilst Father and us, the two boys, were the 'jungli' fraternity with our shikar bonding. Father's grandmother; our great-grandmother, then in her eighties, was a venerable old lady of great grace and dignity. "Ammaji", as she was lovingly called, had brought up Father from his very early childhood with great devotion and care. Father had lost his mother shortly after being born.

Father's initial years were spent at Jalandhar in Punjab, from where he had been sent to Gurukul Kangri near Haridwar, for a spell of schooling. Ammaji, the doting grandmother, called the lonesome grandson 'Deva' for his serious and sensitive nature. For the purposes of these musing, therefore, I would call him "Deva-Pitta" hereafter in this narration- as 'Pitta' (father) is how we children always addressed him.

Deva-Pitta had a few years of schooling at Gurukul Kangri, near Haridwar on the Ganga River. He seems to have thrived on the exposure both physically and the Arya Samaj based traditional educational ambience at the Gurukul. Being located on the Ganga River, enabled him to learn to swim – and he became a powerful swimmer. It was at this time that he developed a great fondness for the jungle and environment around Haridwar. He would

Parents – 1930

sometimes tell us of those early days. He talked often of seeing wild elephants on the other side of the river while swimming, and of a particularly massive and menacing looking tusker who had a single tusk. Deva-Pitta would nostalgically remember the crystal clear streams flowing through green beds of 'Bhrami-booti', in the nearby lush jungles of Chila and Malhan across the River east of Haridwar. The streams flowed out of the lower slopes of the Shivaliks.

Deva-Pitta would in his reminiscent mood recount his first serious shikar episode as a budding, keen shikari. It had taken place in Hoshangabad district – in his second place of posting. A boastful young village malguzar, or landlord (in an attempt to impress), gathered a small crowd of the curious villagers and then led the keen young shikari officer to an abandoned silver mine, located some distance away in the midst of scattered mixed jungle. A path sloped into the depths, the sides being overgrown with foliage and exposed roots of nearby trees. It was claimed that often a leopard or sometimes even a tiger was known to have used the cool, hidden depths of the old mine as a hideout and resting place . Father narrated how he and the crowd of curious onlookers were initially tense and apprehensive of what might emerge from the underground mine. However, complacency soon set in and the atmosphere eased off, as there was no response or reaction from within the dark entrance of the mine, even after several stones had been flung inside. The crowd soon got a bit restive and noisy with the easing of tension.

Deva-Pitta (1945)

The young malguzar, an overly rash and bold man, proceeded to go down into the mine to take a closer look. It was an obvious attempt at showing off and needless bravado. Before he could be dissuaded, the man had lowered himself from a side onto the sloping entrance, luckily still grasping the roots on the sides to do this. Suddenly, there was a loud roar as a tiger emerged from within, passing inches beneath the now petrified man, who was 'pulling himself up' on the roots he was holding on to for dear life to get out of the way. He barely managed to and the tiger made his getaway. Father described to us how loud, awesome and overwhelming the affect of the tiger's sudden roar was, which he said, sounded like the sudden overturning of a big pitcher of water. He said the loud roar struck him like a sudden blow in the stomach. He found himself standing alone awkwardly, with the rifle in his hand, not quite knowing what to do. The villagers

had all scattered, some even having climbed trees or had just vanished. The now thoroughly frightened and sheepish Malguzar and the equally shaken shikari had learnt a lesson. It had been a near thing, but the villagers soon filtered back and later were able to raise a laugh over the incident.

Deva-Pitta was next posted to Chanda (now renamed as Chandrapur, in Maharashtra). It was considered one of the most 'jungli' districts of the then CP. After many abortive attempts, he at last had a successful break when he managed to bag two tigers during the same night while sitting up on a natural kill. The first tiger, a full-grown male, had arrived on the kill after darkness had set in. After letting him feed noisily for a few minutes, Father had taken an unhurried shot with the. 405 calibre rifle. A torch was clamped onto the rifle, which illuminated the feeding tiger and the rifle sight. The recoil of the weapon had unsighted him briefly, for the tiger had disappeared from view after the shot. Vaguely he sensed that the animal had rushed off to the left, the direction he was facing while feeding. Having a wounded tiger around, Father took the prudent decision to wrap himself in a blanket that had been brought along for just this kind of eventuality and tried to get some sleep on the machan.

Wondering what could have gone wrong with the earlier shot, he had dozed off after the day's excitement. He woke up with a start around midnight, on hearing the unmistakable loud tearing sound of the tiger again feeding on the kill. It was baffling that the tiger had come back after being fired at. Father carefully prepared himself noiselessly and again took a shot, after illuminating the feeding tiger, which was facing to the right this time as he lay eating the kill. This time Father hurriedly followed with a hasty snapshot in the dust raised by the tiger – but again when the dust settled, it became clear that the animal had moved away and could not be seen any more from the machan.

During the night, the waiting villagers, from some distance

away, had heard the shot fired earlier in the night and later the two fired in quick succession around midnight. On cautiously approaching next morning, they soon located the midnight tiger, which had barely gone some fifty yards after receiving the heart shot. Elated with this success, Deva-Pitta speculated as to what could have happened earlier in the night, when he had taken the first shot. This led to the sharp-eyed Gond shikaris searching around, until one of them chanced upon some drops of blood along some deep claw marks in the soil, leading away towards the left. The Gond tracker explained that cats do not unsheathe their claws unless in great pain and in the final death throes. More drops of blood were found and further search led to finding this dead tiger where he had fallen after covering more than a hundred yards or so. The tale about the bagging of the two tigers, had been told to us in our childhood days so often that I can reconstruct the story thus.

I was born around this time at Chanda in October 1935. Before me were the two sisters born in January 1932 and May 1934 at Akola and Hoshangabad, respectively. Vijay, the youngest brother, was born at Father's next place of posting, Bhandara in August 1937. This last named place had a great many snakes and I am told that I spoke my first intelligible words on sighting one under the dining table – by exclaiming 'chaap –chaap' ('saamp' or snake). Thereafter, Father was posted to Jabalpur, which was the second most sought after place in the Central Province after Nagpur, the provincial capital at that time.

My earliest memories are of Jabalpur of around 1939, as a four-year-old. Foremost of these was the arrival of a new car in the family, a momentous and very exciting event for us all. It was a maroon coloured 'Morris Eight' with black mudguards. It had then cost Father the princely amount of Rupees 2700/-. The cars headlights, looked like droopy eyes that were built into the front mudguards – a new innovation in those days. Headlights on earlier models were usually mounted perched up on the mudguards. The

car had a sliding roof-top opening, which could be used whenever required. This feature was an instant success with us children, and we would not tire of using this novelty; the all pervading odour of the leather upholstery in the interior of the car; and the smart clicking of the direction 'indicator' arm when activated, with an orange light. And then there was the smart little chrome plated handle that operated the worm-wheel, which would slowly open the front glass wind-shield. All these were a source of great thrill and excitement for us. In the collage of childhood memories, the 'Morris Eight' figures prominently.

The family, including great-grand-mother Ammaji, and our Gond ayah, 'Rukma-bai', drove in the new car – to what was then called 'Kanha-Kisli', a well-known wildlife sanctuary, located in the Mandla district some 200 Kms south of Jabalpur. This was the first ever exposure to seeing wildlife for us children, and we were most excited about it all. I have no memory of that early visit, except the sighting of a tiger during an afternoon drive in the sanctuary. I will try and describe that magic moment as I remember it.

We were all piled up in the Morris car, the four of us children crowding the roof-top opening for viewing the plentiful herds of Chital and Barasingha deer feeding on the abundant yellowed grass in the wide sunlit maidans or meadows of the sanctuary. The Sal forest fringes had these sunlit glades of knee-high yellowing grass, on which the scattered herds of deer were browsing. The smooth gravel forest road enabled the car to get fairly close to the grazing deer, and we children pointed excitedly to the fine antlers of some of the Chital and Barasingha stags. The deer hardly took any notice of us, as we whispered to each other our discoveries. This being our very first exposure to wildlife, Deva-Pitta had been driving slowly to let us savour the breath-taking beauty of the jungle setting fully.

It was a sunlit afternoon, and from the fringe of the Sal jungle, close to the shadows, in the opposite direction from where we were looking, a tiger silently stalked the feeding deer. Rukma-

bai, our Gond Ayah, had first noticed the tiger from her rear seat and there was a ripple of excited loud whispers as the car came to a halt and we all turned our attention towards the animal in full view. The tiger was about seventy-five yards or so from us and seemed to sense that we had seen him, as he quickly turned around and flattened himself for concealment in the grass, to soon melt away into the shadows behind. The memory of that golden moment still lives in my mind's eye.

I had been just four years old in 1939 when the above narrated sighting took place. Later, there were numerous visits to Kanha in the years that followed. The memories of these are overlapping. Some years later, in 1946-47 Deva-Pitta was posted as the Additional District Magistrate, or the district's second-in-command at Mandla, located on the Naramada River. Kanha was located in the Mandla District, and thus plays a very central part in these jungle memories. Later, I will recount other shikar encounters of the period when Deva-Pitta was posted at Mandla (1946-47).

A brief description of the Kanha forests and surroundings, would not be out of place here. The entire region is a part of the Satpura Hills and is truly 'Rudyard Kipling' country – straight from 'Jungle Book'. You will come across names like Seoni, Bichia, Motinala, Wainganga and the Mahadeo Hills. The beauty of the forests in the region have an enchanting quality, quite unsurpassed by any of the jungle places one got to see even in later years. 'Kanha Chronicle', brought out by the Centre for Environment Education, Ahmedabad, describes the Kanha Landscape thus :

> --*All of Kanha lies in the eastern segment of the Satpura's in the Mekal range. The plateaux or 'dadar ', as they are locally called – range from 800 metres to 900 metres above sea level. From their many escarpments one can take in a grand view in one sweep – a miscellany of the wooded slopes and valleys of bamboo and mixed tree , groves of 'Sal', and the rolling meadows.*

The plateaux have scanty tree growth – most fruit bearing like 'achar', 'amla', and 'tendu'- but there is an abundance of grass. Below the plateaux, in the nalas, the vegetation is moist with bamboo and tall mango trees providing shade and coolness. At many places there are rapids and waterfalls, and the water in the streams is crystal clear.

Kanha even today survives as one of the better preserved Project Tiger Reserves in India, and it remains easily the most beautiful area to see undisturbed wildlife. In fact, the Sanctuary has been considerably enlarged in area in the post independence effort to better preserve the tiger and other wildlife. Several villages have been relocated and have been absorbed by the jungle.

Since the Morris Eight car featured in it, there is an event worth recounting pertaining to 'Nawab', the family's russet colored, mixed-retriever pet dog. Nawab seemed to always give and get special attention from Deva-Pitta. On this occasion, a day's trip to Katni, which was some 95 kilometres northeast of Jabalpur, was undertaken in the Morris Eight, accompanied by Kallu Khan, the tall Pathan 'chaprasi' or office peon and Nawab. Katni was connected to Jabalpur by a dusty metalled road. Kallu Khan was to carry the bundle of files and papers tied up in a red cloth and to generally look after Nawab. Katni was, in those days a prominent

INTRODUCING 'DEVA –PITTA' AND HIS SHIKAR EPISODES

centre for processing limestone, and consequently was a messy and dusty place. The Dak bungalow was located on a prominent high ground , in the centre of the limestone kilns scattered area within the town. Father had hoped to complete the work at Katni in time to be able to get back to Jabalpur by nightfall.

Later in the day, when Father returned to the Dak Bungalow to collect Kalu Khan and Nawab for the return journey, the dog was missing. Kalu Khan had been under the impression that Nawab had gone with the Sahib in the car. Recrimination was pointless, and a frantic search began. After a few hours a report came in that a police constable had seen the 'Magistrate Sahibs' dog going along the road to Jabalpur. The constable claimed that he had even tried to catch the dog, but Nawab had growled at him, even baring his teeth and evading capture had just kept going. Indeed, in the few hours, Nawab had trudged many miles along the dusty road on his way home to Jabalpur. Deva-Pitta found him later that night, limping along the road-side, his feet badly lacerated owing to the rough road surface. It remained a mystery as to how he had found the road leading to Jabalpur from Katni. Somehow, Nawab had thought he had been left behind and had decided to go 'home' to Jabalpur on his own.

It was considered a dangerous undertaking in those days to travel on the Katni – Jabalpur road at night as it passed through some recognized dacoit-infested 'thugee' country. The famous English policeman , Major General Sleeman had crushed the dacoit menace in the mid-nineteenth century in this very area and had resettled some of the miscreants and their families in a place named after him as Saleemanabad, which was located close to the road leading to Katni. After finding Nawab, Father prudently spent the night at a wayside police station, and got back safely to Jabalpur and home the next day. With this incident Nawab became more than just a hero with us all.

JABALPUR – KASHMIR AND NAGPUR

Jabalpur was an elaborate cantonment town. Well spread out and neatly kept, it also had a grass airfield just behind the Deputy Commissioner's bungalow. We once saw a demonstration flight of a 'Wapiti' Royal Indian Air Force aircraft at this airfield. The biplane had to have its propeller hand-cranked for starting up and I remember seeing the pilot struggling with the task, the chin-strap of his leather helmet, flapping loosely in the wind. On his forehead he wore the goggles as they were characteristically worn in those days. The 'Wapiti' had started with a coughing roar, blowing and flatenning the grass behind in the slipstream. The Second World War was just beginning and the British War propaganda was just starting.

'V' for victory silver badges were distributed for us children, and military flag marches carried out in the Sadar Bazar area. There was a Scottish Battalion in the station, quite noticeable in their dark kilts and boat-shaped side-caps with a red 'cherry' in the middle and a short tail hanging behind. The distinctive Kilt uniform was often visible in the Bazar area next to the Cantonment. British, or 'white,' troops were commonly referred to as 'gora-paltan' in Hindustani.

I remember seeing one of the flag marches with the 'gora-paltan' men taking part, wearing khaki shorts and field service packs on their backs. The steel helmets or tin hats, worn in a jaunty and cocky manner and their Lee-Enfield service rifles slung with the muzzle end pointing downwards. The conspicuous swagger of the marching columns with wailing pipes and drums band being led by a band-major, wielding a silver mace – walking as if he owned the world, excluding an air of supreme confidence. It was heady stuff and most certainly captured my childhood fancy.

The Second World War had just started in far away Europe, the Japanese joining in some two years later. My impression is that the British colonial rulers at that time went about their business in a fairly laid-back manner at Jabalpur. There was a general air of confidence that was so visible in the 'Devil may care' look of the marching troops that swept past us – swinging their well tattooed arms with un-mistaken pride in themselves. The War was to last for six long years.

Another episode at Jabalpur occurred sometime in 1939 or 1940 . Deva-Pitta was assigned the task as magistrate on duty to receive the prominent national leaders arriving by trains at the Jabalpur Railway Station. The Indian National Congress was holding some big gathering at Jabalpur at that time. Our mother accompanied Father, who took sister Kamla and youngest brother Vijay, fondly called 'Chotu', along on the occasion. Mother had carried a bouquet of fresh flowers from our garden for receiving the much admired Mahatma Gandhi who was arriving that day at the railway station. All went well and the flowers were duly presented by our mother to the Mahatma. Young brother 'Chotu' earned a big smile and hug from Gandhiji, but when they turned to leave, 'Chotu' asked the Mahatma to please return his mother's flowers. The way the great man handled the little child with a gracious smile, remains a very treasured moment in the family's bank of memories.

Father was posted in early 1942 to the provincial capital at Nagpur. Before taking up his new appointment, he was granted four months leave from April, during which the family journeyed

up the country for a memorable holiday in Kashmir. Enroute, I have faint memories of brief stopovers at Agra, Delhi, Jalandhar, Batala and Lahore before reaching Jammu by train. Thereafter we travelled by bus over the Banihal Pass route to initially stay in a cottage on Dr Mathura Das's estate on the Gupkar Road. Upslope was located the Shankrachariya Temple whose bell could be faintly heard. The blended fragrance of the wild flowers on the slopes of the hill as we climbed up the path, remains embedded with nostalgia as a part of childhoods precious memories. Later, we floated down the Jhelum in a houseboat to Gandherbal, where we were then moored to the bank of the river besides a grove of stately Chinar trees. Later, we had a few days stay at Gulmarg, which included a climb up to Khilanmarg. Then a stay at Pahelgam in a cottage tent whilst the parents trekked upto the Amarnath Shrine. All in all a most beautiful dreamlike and most memorable interlude in the valley.

1942 – Kashmir – Ganderbal

Vijay, Kamala, Meera and Self
Khilan Marg

Nagpur, the provincial capital, was quite anti-climatic after Jabalpur and the holiday in Kashmir. In early 1943 our great-grandmother 'Ammaji' passed away suddenly. She was the heart centre of our family, and her passing away left us mourning and grieving. At Nagpur the 'Morris Eight' was sold, fetching almost double the amount paid by Deva-Pitta when it was bought at Jabalpur. An 'Austin –Seven' of an earlier vintage was bought to fill the void.

The 'Austin Seven' was bought second-hand and was an earlier model than the 'Morris Eight'. It was a two-door box like sedan, with thin motorcycle tyres and the spare wheel located on the rear of the car. It could be started with a crank handle that was permanently left hanging in front of the engine. Even I, as an eight-year-old, could with some effort crank the suspended handle to start the car. The 'Austin' soon became a favourite with us as Father started using it occasionally for his tours to visit the subdivisions of the Nagpur District allotted to him. One of

these was Katol Tehsil, which was well known for the oranges grown there. Its Tehsil Headquarters was located at Katol, a small town, which was some 70 kilometres from Nagpur on the trunk railway line leading northwards, and was also connected with a dusty metalled road which ran adjacent to the railway line. Father would use either mode of travel for his tours towards Katol. When the 'Austin' was used, some of us amongst the children would gleefully accompany if it was over the weekend or when there was a holiday from school.

    The 'Austin Seven' seemed to have a sturdy engine, for I do not recollect it giving us any problem during our outings. It had mechanical brakes which were not very effective and the drill was that we passengers, including Sheikh Imam, the one-eyed peon, would hurriedly get off the slow moving car to help in physically holding the car back and not letting it gather too much speed on a slope. We would try to hold back the car by dragging one foot on the ground while keeping the other foot on the narrow footboard. There were several places on the road to Katol which had the road sloping significantly at both sides of the nala being crossed. On one occasion, I remember that inspite of our efforts of slowing the little car, it gained excessive speed on the downslope approach of a nala. As the speeding car got to the low spillway, there was a resounding metallic crack as the main leaf spring broke. It led to some delay, but we resorted to some Improvisation by getting hold of a piece of wood to use as a splint to hold the broken spring in place with bits of wire and some rope. Thereafter, we managed to get to Katol by limping along to cover the remaining distance.

    Another interesting thing pertaining to the 'Austin' was the attention it would receive from a white cow on the road leading to a manganese mining town enroute to Katol. On seeing the car, the cow would raise her tail high and give chase every time we went that way. We would cheer loudly for 'Daddy' to speed up the struggling little car. Often the cow would give up the chase after

'jittering' us closely, but once she succeeded in butting us hard on the rear spare wheel, which seemed to help us go a little faster. The cow thereafter gave up the chase abruptly and stood looking at the receding car with a bewildered expression. This particular cow seemed to find the sound of the Austin engine irritating and invariably gave chase.

Once an amusing incident occurred when Namdeo, the curly haired man-servant, sat in the driver's seat, handling the steering wheel and gear shift as if he was driving the car as children at play often do. Namdeo had been washing the car that day, and in a rash and misplaced moment of mischief, I engaged the starting handle and gave it a push. To my horror the engine started up with a gasping sigh and Namdeo' took off' by releasing the clutch - the car being in gear, just lurched forward. The next twenty minutes or so, with Namdeo on the wheel, was a hair-raising winding in and out within and amongst the grove of wild date palm trees that grew scattered in abundance in the area, each tree a few yards from the other. Namdeo, sitting low in the driver's seat, was a picture of concentration on the steering wheel and it was a miracle that he somehow evaded hitting any of the trees and finally came to an abrupt halt when one of the front wheels got trapped in a brick-lined drain in front of the house and the engine stalled. We had watched helplessly, holding our breath, during the episode and realized how close we had come to a disaster. Later we saw the slapstick humour in the event. It was a real 'Laurel and Hardy' scene – but it was a very close call.

Before the 'Austin Seven' drives out on its motorcycle-thin tyred wheels from these collection of childhood memories , there was a ghastly accident that took place at Nagpur with it that I remember. A tonga pony whilst negotiating a blind corner, somehow collided violently with the car. On impact, with all the weight of the laden tonga behind him, the pony got impaled on the car door handle. The enormous outflow of blood from the

ghastly injury on his neck was a sickening sight and the stricken animal just bled to death before our eyes. This sad last memory of our otherwise happy memories of our toy-like 'Austin' gets a bit blemished by this last event.

Nagpur was a frightfully hot place in summer. The parched countryside would quite simmer in the heat. The bungalows would have a couple of rooms cooled by having thick 'khus-tatis' fitted on all openings which had to be frequently splashed with water from the outside. The hot air would cool down a bit by the evaporation whilst passing through the *'khas-tuti'*. Electric fans had not yet come into general use , so in keeping with the colonial culture of the time, a *'pankha-wala'* boy sat outside pulling the rope that gave the suspended 'pankha' a to and fro motion. The heat was quite oppressive and it would take some time in the evening for it to cool down.

The parched black cotton soil would develop cracks owing to the heat. Finally, to dispel the exhaustion in the air the long-awaited monsoon would set in with a thundering downpour, which often lasted for a couple of days. One fine morning like a touch of magic, the whole countryside would turn a beautiful shade of fresh, almost luminous green everywhere. The croaking of frogs seemed to resume to fill the place with a long-awaited ambience. We children would hunt for the red velvet bugs that would emerge. The coming of monsoon at Nagpur was indeed a very special something that memory holds on to.

NAGPUR – THE JHILPA MAN-EATER LEOPARD

After the earlier exposure to the beauty of the evergreen, dense forests of Kanha-Kisli, during our stay in Jabalpur, the scattered patches of teak forests in the Nagpur area looked comparatively bare and unattractive.

However, during the monsoons, the large teak leaves would sprout and the fresh greenery would be quite fulsome and change the appearance of the countryside completely.

During the prolonged, very dry summer months, the deciduous teak jungle had been quite threadbare for cover. The carpet of fallen dry leaves made loud crackling sound, and silent movement in such forests was almost impossible. In the district, most of the area seemed to have such teak jungle that grew at places on the slopes and re-entrants of low lying and flat, barren hills. The area of Deva-Pitta's Katol and Soaner Tehsils, was mainly like this. The jungle, being too bare, seemed to contain hardly any wildlife.

It was, however, surprising that there were a fair number of panthers or leopards in the area. Known by both the names, usually the 'leopard' means the bigger more powerfully built jungle dwellers. These predators had adapted themselves to the surroundings in a remarkable manner, poaching on the village cattle, goats and dogs. There was however fairly dense cover in the seasonal dry nalas, which often had some residual pools of stagnant water, which was used to advantage by these clever animals. Living close to the human population in the villages, made these big cats very bold and cheeky.

At one place a leopard had cleverly taken to always leaving his kills hanging safely on a high branch on a tree, so that vultures and other scavengers could not get to it. It was revealing to see how this particular leopard would secure the kill on a fairly high branch of a tree. Deva-Pitta tried to shoot this animal by sitting up on a machan on an adjacent tree. The wily leopard saw the shikari as his attention was on the tree tops where his kill was suspended. Deva-Pitta got a fleeting glimpse of the wily animal looking up at him in the machan before he melted away. On another occasion the same cheeky leopard picked up a small village cur from under the string bed on which Deva-Pitta was resting at night in the open near one of the village huts.

This particular village was in the centre of a saucer-like shallow valley, ringed with some mixed forest and scrub. Several hung up and abandoned dried kills, which had turned black, were visible on the trees at several places.

Deva-Pitta was assigned Katol and Saoner Tehsils in his care, and both these lay northwest and north of Nagpur respectively. Further upcountry to the north lay the Mahadeo Hills of the Satpuras in which were the neighboring districts of Betul and Chindwara. The Chindwara area was then being used as the jungle warfare training area by the British for the war raging in Burma against the Japanese. The trunk railway line leading north from Nagpur, initially slants diagonally towards Katol in a north-westerly direction before turning due north entering the hilly jungle terrain towards Betul. Katol and Saoner Tehsils were well known for oranges, 'Nagpur Oranges' being famously known countrywide. The orange groves, each covering several acres, were generally rectangular, with dense, dark green foliage of the ten-foot- high trees planted in neat rows. The orange groves were irrigated with the help of a bullock-drawn, primitive system called

NAGPUR – THE JHILPA MAN-EATER LEOPARD

'rehat,' which consisted of two bullocks being so yoked that they pulled a large buffalo hide 'bucket' of water from the well over a wooden pulley. The 'bucket' would empty out into the channels irrigating the orange trees. The bullocks would then shuffle backwards for the next effort. The orange groves were a scattered few, generally adjacent to nullah beds owing to the water table allowing wells being dug for irrigating the orange groves.

Generally, the Nagpur area was very dry and mainly rain-fed. The crop was mainly 'Jawar', somewhat like maize, and in those days was the staple food-grain in the region. The Jawar fields, resembling the tall growth of maize, were raided by large flocks of parakeets during the day and wild pigs and nilgais during the night. Almost all large fields had machans, propped up on stout poles that provide an elevated platform for the watchman to drive away flocks of raiding birds with the use of a well-aimed sling shot accompanied by a loud yell. For the wild pigs and nilgai besides the sling-shot pellets, empty tins were sometimes put up in a manner that these could be pulled during the night with a grass rope to make some noise to drive away the raiders.

Within the first few months of our stay at Nagpur, Father had bagged a leopard by using the well known method of sitting up on a machan over a bleating goat. It was recognized that he was a budding shikari.

The first vague reports that Deva-Pitta got of the Jhilpa Man-eater were followed by a fresh and bold attempt by the leopard to climb up a machan in a jowar field by using the horizontal 'ballis' on a side used for climbing onto the platform by the watchman. The watchman had been fast asleep wrapped up in a rough blanket, which also covered his head. The leopard obviously knew of the victims presence on the machan from the earlier noises made by the watchman to drive away raiding pigs and nilgai. The leopard biding his time, climbed up the machan by stealth and made a grab at the sleeping watchman's throat. Providentially, the rough

blanket saved the man as the attacker grabbed the blanket and in his getaway, jumped off the machan, with the blanket in his mouth. The suddenly woken and frightened watchman hastily grabbed an axe and a sickle that he had with him with which he managed to make enough noise to deter the killer from renewing his murderous attempt.

The report of this incident reached the District Headquarters and the Deputy Commissioner, the district head, asked Father to proceed to the village named Jhilpa, camp there and try to shoot the maneater. Already, the leopard had killed about eighty people from Jhilpa and the other villages around it. Most of the victims were taken at night and the whole area was quite terrorized by the activities of this predator. During day time the leopard did not normally molest anyone. However, there had been an attack on a young goatherd, a boy of about fourteen, who was mauled on his back badly at evening time. He escaped as the axe he had on his shoulder got in the leopard's way as he tried to grab his neck. Some people in the fields in the vicinity raised an alarm and the leopard abandoned his attack.

Thus, during the summer of 1943, the man-eater held sway in the village of Jhilpa and surrounding hamlets . The area was held in the grip of terror by the man-eater leopard of Jhilpa which operated mainly at night. Jhilpa was located some 16 Kilometres northeast of Katol, the Tehsil Headquarters. Since it was within the sub-division of the district assigned to my Father, he got drawn into an official effort of destroying the dangerous animal. Deva-Pitta's experience was limited as he had until then shot a leopard or two. But tackling a man-eater was new for him. Only later the exploits of the great shikari Jim Corbett got wide publicity. His books 'Man-eaters of Kumaon' and 'The Rudraprayag Man-eating Leopard', became bestsellers. In his writing he had analysed the reason why tigers and leopards/panthers take to man-eating.

NAGPUR – THE JHILPA MAN-EATER LEOPARD

In 1943, it was a completely different and unknown field of endeavour for Deva-Pitta. The risks involved and the gravity of the challenge of tackling the wily leopard, only emerged later as Father grappled with the problem of coming to grips with the task. Initially, trying to locate the elusive leopard seemed like looking for the proverbial needle in the haystack. It would seem in hindsight that Deva-Pitta approached the task as if it was just another panther or leopard and he would adopt the known methods to tackle it. At first he did not realize the risks for him and his staff in staying in a tented camp near the village.

The Second World War was at its height at the time, and the local problems and issues received comparatively lesser notice and publicity. The depredations of the Man-eater of Jhilpa were consequently not publicized and thus not widely known. Owing to the ongoing war, petrol was rationed and all movement away from the railway was performed by bullock carts.

A lighter bullock cart version with smaller wheels was called 'rengi', which could carry just one passenger besides the driver of the cart. The passenger sat astride, facing forward behind the driver. The next bigger version was a medium sized cart which carried several passengers who sat sideways facing inwards. These carts had a bamboo matting hood, which allowed you to see forwards over the bobbing heads of the bullocks or towards the rear through the open end. Some hay covered with a 'duree' provided a bit of a cushion, but the cart ride was an uncomfortable affair. There being no springs, the wooden framework jolted you along, letting your spine absorb the rude shocks. A sandy nala bed would be a temporary relief with the wheels making a pleasant grinding sound, and the bumps would cease until you crossed the nala onto the stony far side.

Deva-Pitta moved to Jhilpa ahead, to getting on with the effort. I was to follow a few days later with Sheikh Imam, once my school closed down for the summer break. Father had by then realized

that he had grossly under- estimated the risk involved in the task in hand. He had found that to live in a tented camp with his staff at Jhilpa was quite unrealistic and dangerous.

Secondly, I was to soon join him at Jhilpa after he had been there for a few days. Father realized the grave risk in having me, an eight year old on hand but could not somehow, send word for stopping my joining him.

As per the pre-arranged plan I got to Katol along with Sheikh Imam by train. Sheikh Imam was Father's all purpose 'chaprasi' (peon) and camp cook. He was blind in one eye, owing to smallpox in his childhood. He had stayed behind at Nagpur to bring me along with him, once my school holidays commenced.

We got to Jhilpa by evening, having travelled by bullock cart after the train journey to Katol. It was a blistering hot summer, and the cart travel was a jarring experience. The tented camp was in a shady spot under a large banyan tree. However, the village elders had by then drawn Father's attention to the grave risk from the man-eater of living in the camp. The village school, the only brick building in the village, had been vacated for our use for sleeping purposes, the school having a summer break. The tented camp was comfortable and cool and safe during the day. The reign of terror of the man-eater would set in as the evening descended. We would move into the school building for the night.

The very first night after Sheikh Imam and I had joined Father at Jhilpa, the prevailing tension was all pervading. However, I was too excited and happy having joined Father.

The method being employed by Father was to carry out short beats in likely patches of the scrub forest in the re-entrants in the vicinity of Jhilpa and other villages in the area. It was a wild guessing effort, but after many days of futile efforts, a leopard was flushed out when two adjacent re-entrants were to be beaten, one at a time with a common machan being used. Mistakenly, the second re-entrant beaters started off prematurely and the leopard

came up from the second beat emerging from behind Father, who was still facing the other way.

Deva-Pitta chanced to look back over his shoulder, realizing that the second beat had also started, and found himself looking straight into the face of a large leopard staring up at him in the machan from about 50 yards distance. The leopard made a quick getaway before Father could turn around for a shot with his rifle. This had happened a few days before we joined Deva-Pitta at Jhilpa. It was definitely a missed chance. There was however no way of knowing if it was the man-eater or just another of the numerous leopards in the area.

Several times Father sat up on a machan over a bleating goat at some select place in the evenings. The man-eater had probably been fired at earlier in such efforts by local shikaris, and did not respond. However, it was very risky and dangerous for him and the party of locals with him to get back after dark. The bright beam of the three cell torch may have deterred the leopard somewhat. Deva-Pitta realized the gravity of the matter and reduced these attempts.

After I had joined father, the routine was roughly that in the morning hours two to three beats were carried out in the selected re-entrants. The machans were already put up there from the previous attempts. Once, in one such beat, there was sudden excitement when a hyena broke cover and dashed past us. In another beat, there was some commotion when one of the beaters caught a young hare. I tried to keep the little furry creature in the tent, but he must have been hurt when he was caught, for by that evening it did not survive.

* * * * *

The village of Jhilpa had a prominent dry nala on its northern side. The nala sides was full of dense cover of scrub and some

trees. At some places some pools of stagnant water still survived the intense heat. The nala was evidently used by the man-eater for the advantage it provided with a covered approach to the village. Further upstream and well away was our tented camp.

We were by now fully aware of the danger the nala posed for us in the tented camp. It was the main reason that the villagers had insisted on us and our small party of supporting staff to daily move into the village school building for the night. Accordingly, the drill became that every evening we would get settled in the school building before it got dark and the curfew imposed by the dreaded killer set in The village school-building was a modest two-or three-small room affair, which had a verandah enclosed with a sturdy wooden lattice. Thorn bushes had been strongly wedged in the openings both above and below the lattice screen to make it safe and deter the man-eater from entering. Owing to the summer heat, Father and I would sleep on *charpoys* (string beds) in the enclosed verandah. Beyond the verandah, there was a man-high boundary wall enclosing the area within which the schools classes were held.

Jhilpa village and most of the other hamlets around, were a cluster of untidy mud plastered huts, having hand made sun baked mud tiles for the roofs. Jhilpa was the largest village of about a hundred huts, located beside the seasonal nala mentioned earlier. Shady trees beside the nala helped in preserving the water in several stagnant but clean water pools in the nala. The scrub beside the nala provided ideal cover for the man-eater to approach the village.

Sometimes the man-eater was known to have had attempted breaking into the flimsy huts for securing his human kills. But the stifling heat drove people to sleep in the verandahs, from where it was possible for the panther to secure his victims by stealth. Consequently there was hardly any family that had not suffered at the hands of the dreaded killer over the many years.

The village dogs would set up baying by which the village population would try to guess the latest location of the predator. I remember one such night, when Father had still not come back from sitting up over a bleating goat, and the kerosene lantern after some hiccups just blew off, I lay in bed, petrified, listening to the village dogs in our neighborhood barking away.

I was staring through the safety of the lattice screen at the outside boundary which in the darkness seemed to grow menacingly into imaginary shapes. Luckily, Father's return and Sheikh Imam's re-lighting the lantern was just in time to dispel the frightening time that I was having. For an eight-year old, the fearsome spell that held the village in its grip had its imagined and real affect on me. I told Deva-Pitta that I had seen a dark shape on the boundary wall just before he had come back that night. The barking of the village dogs and the wailing of jackals filled the night with a kind of terror that gave everyone a wide-eyed expression, and people conversed in whispers. Father's strong torch light searched the surroundings.

After the novelty of being with Father had worn off a bit, I was a terribly scared eight year old child cowering with fear of things in the darkness. It was a harrowing experience and sometimes I felt that Father was beginning to regret having me on hand. The strenuous routine of frequently sitting up over a live, bleating goat and the daily attempts at beating likely patches of jungle were beginning to have its affect on him.

One morning we had just completed beating a patch of scrub-covered high ground, which had on an earlier occasion produced some excitement when a hyena had dashed past us. As we were descending from the machan, I drew Father's attention to someone having rushed up on a village pony to where our bullock carts were waiting down slope to take us for the next beat. We hurried down and met the messenger halfway, who breathlessly broke the news that a leopard had been sighted by the village women in the

scrub jungle in the nala upstream of where our tents were pitched.

Some beaters had been collected to drive the leopard further upstream for which a machan had already been put up in a suitable tree. It was a rough and bumpy ride to the spot in the bullock cart. The plan of action to beat the scrub jungle where the leopard had been seen was finalized. The beaters assembled near our tented camp, and Father, with me following, silently took a slight detour to the machan. The leopard was still reported in the undergrowth upstream along the nala .

Father and I climbed into the machan and after some time the beat to drive the leopard towards us began. The leopard was expected to be driven upstream along the dry nala which continued to have patchy cover on both sides. About 200 yards further up from our machan was a prominent, thick- trunked mango tree. A young man as a backup stop quickly climbed this tree on Father's last minute suggestion. Adjacent to the mango tree on the far bank was an orange grove.

The beat commenced when we were quite ready. Nothing happened for some time and just as we were thinking that it was yet another blank, a leopard appeared walking almost nonchalantly along the faint game trail beside the dry nala bed. He did not seem bothered or alarmed at the noise and din around him. As he passed beneath us, in the couple of seconds of the opportunity of taking a shot with the .405 Winchester rifle offered itself to Father; there was an unexpected mix-up owing to an obstructing branch. It all happened so quickly that we got somewhat nonplussed for a few seconds. Meanwhile the leopard carried on and when the noise of the beat began to subside behind him, he sat down on his haunches like a dog under the very mango tree on which Father had placed the stop.

What happened next was quite unplanned. After getting down quickly from the machan, Father tried to stalk the leopard.

From the ground level only the top of the animal's head was

visible as he continued to sit on his haunches, but now showing signs of restlessness under the mango tree. The stop on the mango tree branch remained undetected by the leopard. He kept gesticulating that the leopard was still sitting beneath the mango tree. While the beaters were milling around in a hush, uncertain as to what to do next, Father tried to move towards the leopard with the cocked rifle in his hand. The top of the leopard's head was still visible, but was too small a target to engage. While Father tried to get a clearer view to take an accurate shot, the restive beaters were beginning to become noisy and suddenly the animal took alarm and leapt up into the orange grove and tried to flee the area. The beaters on their own had split up on both sides of the dry nala and were rushing to cut off the leopard's escape.

Meanwhile, Father hurriedly handed over the rifle to Sheikh Imam, who was holding me with the other hand, and grabbed the twelve bore shotgun from him. The twelve bore shotgun was loaded with buck shot. In the wild melee that followed the shotgun was a better weapon for the fleeting task. The rifle handed over to Sheikh Imam was still cocked and in his haste Father had hurriedly turned his attention towards dealing with the leopard.

Suddenly the rifle in Sheikh Imam's hand went off with a loud bang. Mercifully, the barrel was pointing skyward and the shot did no harm to anyone. However, the loud report acted like a starter pistol to set off the beaters in a wild chase to cut off the leopard's escape. One of the beaters carrying a muzzle-loader also let fly with a wild shot in the orange grove, which managed to turn the leopard back towards the nala. The leopard was now panicking and snarling, emitting-blood curdling growls as he re-entered the nala. Fortunately, when it broke cover this time, Father's shotgun rang out and knocked the animal down as he leapt across the dry nala.

The infuriated and excited villagers, just rushed onto the fallen leopard and literally tore him to bits in a frenzy. What had been

a beautiful jungle predator a few minutes before was reduced to a pulpy mass of gore and mud.

* * * * *

We had been very lucky that there had been no accident as things had gone quite uncontrolled. In his final moments in trying to flee, the leopard had even grabbed one of the beater's axe from the crowd and had bitten into the handle before he died.

The accidental setting off of the rifle could have been a disaster, if it had been pointing any other way but sky-wards. As it was, with the beaters milling around, the rifle was a unsuitable weapon with dangerous possibilities of an accident. The shotgun blast had adequately served the purpose.

For me, the whole episode was a thrilling event to be long remembered and relived in later years. It had been my first exposure to the excitement of the hunt. For the first time I had seen a beautiful leopard in the jungle – a never to be forgotten sight. It was, however, upsetting to see the upsurge of emotions of the local people who had lost their dear ones to the man-eater over the years. With tears of anger flowing down their faces they vented their pent-up feelings on the dead, dreaded enemy.

The affect on a hapless population of living with terror, who lived every night with the fear that the man-eater might strike any time, created a haunted look amongst the people. The old and the young, touching Fathers feet in gratitude, as the beaters carried him shoulder high back to the camp was a moving sight.

In Jhilpa and the other hamlets around, the villagers believed that the dreaded man-eater leopard had been shot. There was much celebration in which we also joined in. However, Father tried to convey to the simple villagers that the leopard that had been shot was a young animal and thus may not be the man-eater. He told them in Marathi not to lower their guard as he believed

the man-eater was a wily, old animal. When the next few nights passed off without any further mishap or event, the hope spread that the animal shot in the nala was the man-eater after all.

We stayed on for a few more days and also started to hope that the man-eater had indeed been accounted for. Father decided to wind up the camp and move back to Katol to catch the train back home to Nagpur. The tented camp was moved and set up enroute for us to move back. We slept peacefully that night on the camp cots in our tented camp on our way back to Katol, having moved from Jhilpa in bullock carts.

* * * * *

At sunrise next morning, there was a man standing outside the 'chick' covering the tents opening. There was a forlorn expression on the man's face as he told us that during the previous night, a woman had been killed and dragged out of the village in Jhilpa. The man had hastened on a 'rengi' cart to tell us of this sad news. The woman was a young mother and was sleeping next to her infant child on one side and her own mother on the other side. They were sleeping on the mud plastered floor of their village hut verandah.

We hastened back to Jhilpa and were taken to the scene of the crime. The leopard had somehow made his way through a rough screen of twigs forming a palisade enclosing the space where the family of three were asleep. He had stealthily caught the victim in such a manner that it left the infant sleeping on one side and the older woman on the other side undisturbed. The leopard managed to first kill the woman by strangling her and then proceeded to pull her body through the screen of twigs. He was dragging the dead victim along in the dusty space between the huts when someone who had got up to relieve himself saw the man-eater and raised a hue and cry which aroused the whole village. The early riser had

chanced upon the horrible sight in the faint moonlit night. The leopard had dropped the dead victim and fled into the night.

When we got back to Jhilpa, the villagers had still not disturbed the telltale marks at the scene of the crime. It shook me on seeing the dead woman with the horrible fang marks that had penetrated one of her eyes and under the chin to silently throttle and choke the victim to death. The red and blue marks on her face made me sick and Father had to pull me away from the horrible sight.

The horror of seeing death with all the accompanying anticlimax of finding that the man-eater was still at large, struck like a blow. The earlier misplaced euphoria of having shot the leopard in the nala, being the man-eater proved wrong. Deva-Pitta had been right all along that the wily killer was a larger and older animal, as his pug marks showed.

We stayed on for a few more days, trying every possible thing to get at the killer. Nothing seemed to work, so quite disheartened, we trudged back in the bullock carts –bumping and grinding our way back to the railhead at Katol. Father had exhausted the time he had been told to undertake for the task. However, he promised the village elders that he will come back as soon as he could. He was wiser now that it was not prudent to have an eight-year- old son with him.

* * * * *

Deva-Pitta could only get back to Jhilpa after the rains had abated. This time he just had Sheikh Imam, the cook-cum-peon for looking after him. The villagers had provided a safe place for him to stay on the outskirts of the village. The man-eater had struck more than once in Jhilpa and the surrounding hamlets during the rainy season.

At last there was a break when the man-eater killed a donkey belonging to the village 'kumhar' or mud pot maker. The leopard had made the kill in an orange grove somewhat removed from the village. It seemed likely that the leopard would return to this

kill as it was believed that carnivora are exceptionally fond of horse or in this case donkey's flesh. It is believed it has almost an intoxicating effect on the carnivores animals.

An orange tree was used to prepare a hide with a machan in it. It was well concealed but dangerously low. The orange trees inner branches had to be cut and stout branches were used to build the machan on. However, it was a very risky proposition sitting up for the man-eater as he operated at night and if he should sense Father's presence in the low and flimsy machan, things could go against him. Deva-Pitta was quite conscious of the grave risk he was taking, but decided to have a try. Father was also handicapped that the torch cells were nearly exhausted, and only gave a faint glimmer of light before fading out completely. Owing to the War, torch cells were in short supply.

Since the kill was in an isolated place well away from the noisy village, Deva-Pitta felt that there was every possibility of the leopard making an exception and coming back to the kill. Care had been taken to have only the barest minimum activity in setting up the machan in the orange tree. Father was satisfied with the concealment aspect, as it was crucial that the wily killer did not get suspicious. Father climbed into the hide by late afternoon, and settled down for the vigil. Father saw that Sheikh Imam was carrying his deadly looking 'Rampuri' knife with which he would decapitate the chicken before cooking. Father took the knife from Sheikh Imam as a close defence measure in event of trouble.

Father narrated to us how he could hear the sound of the wooden bells around the cattles necks as they ambled home for the evening, raising dust that hung around the village, and mixed with the blue smoke from the fires that were lit for the evening cooking. He said "Normally, dusk is the most peaceful hour of the day. He felt that the leopard, if he did come to the kill, would do so only after everything settled down for the night. Later, dusk faded into night and a quiet spread over the countryside."

Nothing happened until about 8:30 , when a jackal gave out a loud 'pheau' alarm call, some 300 yards away from the direction the leopard was expected to come from. This was shortly followed by the agitated baiting by a pair of red wattled lapwings, asking the question loudly, "did you do it –did you do it". This bird is called 'titehari' in Hindustani, and even at night warns of any movement close to its nest, which is on the ground. From the direction and distance of the jackal's alarm call and the lapwing's noisy warning, gave Father some time to ease his limbs and set himself up in such a manner that he did not have to move much to take a shot. The canny ability of a leopard, and particularly so of a man-eater, cannot be understated. It was well that Father had done all the right things before the leopard arrived on the kill.

Mercifully everything went well and the leopard started eating the kill when Father's rifle shot was taken with the torch light, which came on dimly for a few seconds. The torch light went off with the recoil of the rifle. Father sat clutching Shiek Imam's dagger in his hand in the darkness.

After some minutes he heard the leopard getting very sick and making a grumbling sound in pain. He appeared to have got away about a hundred yards or so from the kill after being shot. This allowed Father to relax a bit. The villagers, making much noise and carrying 'mashals'(lit fagots), came and took him down from his precarious perch.

Early next morning a villager ran in with the news that a large leopard was lying dead some distance from the orange tree machan. Indeed, it was the Man-eater of Jhilpa, who had at last been made to pay for the terror and havoc he had created over the years in the area.

*****

I would like to add a postscript to the story just narrated. I had been just eight years old at that time, but the events described remain deeply embedded in my memory. I had some doubts about

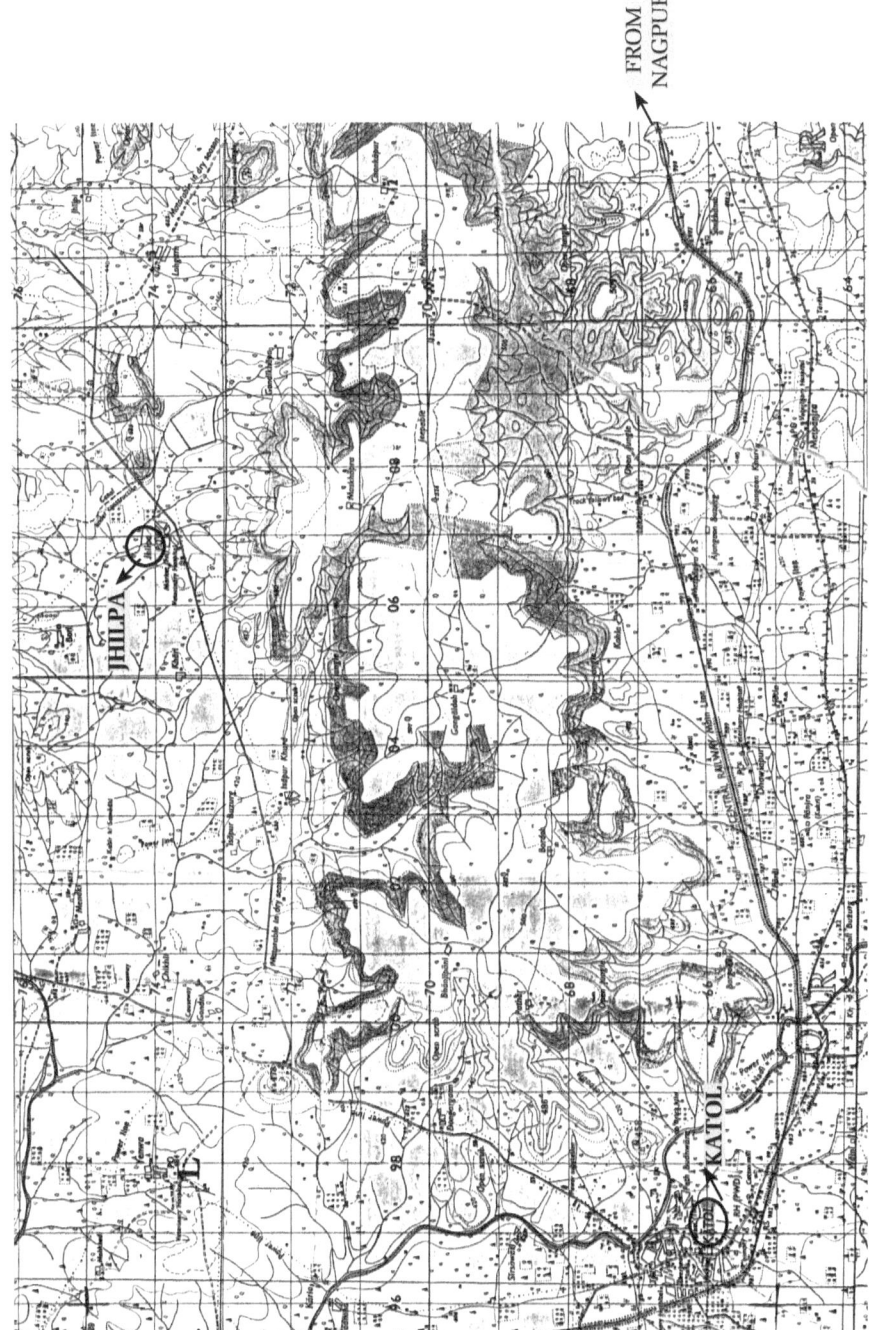

Map of Katol and Jhilpa

the terrain around Jhilpa, but when the Brigadier Commandant of the Brigade of Guards Regimental Centre, located at Kamti near Nagpur sent me a one inch map of Katol and Jhilpa area, I was most surprised that my memory of the place was as the map showed it.

Inspite of the horror and terror in tackling a dreaded killer, what has remained in my mind is the beauty of the young leopard as he had walked past us nonchalantly in the beat. A panther or leopard is the most graceful animal in the Indian jungle. The yellow eyes quite match the colouring of the spotted big cat, which is as wily and clever as he is beautiful. As a man-eater he is uncannily cunning and bold. Operating mainly after dark, the terror he inspires is difficult to comprehend until you have seen it for yourself. As a child it left a deep impression on me.

Deva-Pitta, my Father, was the heroic central figure in the events. I had seen him coolly knocking the leopard down in the nala beat, inspite of the utter confusion that was prevailing. Having been brought up in his younger days in Akola, he spoke Marathi fluently. This was a great asset as a young magistrate and civil servant. The villagers seemed to realize that the 'sahib', was at times exposing himself to great danger whilst trying to tackle the man-eater. The admiration and affection they bestowed on him was most touching.

MANDLA — 1946

By the end of 1945, Father got posted to Bilaspur in Chhattisgarh, as the Additional District Magistrate (ADM). It was not a very pleasant stay owing to us children each having several bouts of malaria. The schooling also was not satisfactory. Father was shifted within a few months to Mandla, to take over in the same appointment in that district.

'Mandla Fort' had been a stronghold of the Gond Rajas in the past. The district town was located on the right bank of the Narbada River. Bilaspur was in fact an adjacent district. The area between Mandla, Bilaspur and the then Princely state of Rewa were the most densely forested at the time. The Rivers Narbada, Sone and Mahanadi originate from the watershed around Amarkantak, each flowing in different directions. The Narbada flows westwards past Mandla and later Jabalpur to eventually drain into the Arabian Sea. The Sone flows north to join the Ganga in Bihar. The third, River Mahanadi in turn drains south-eastward through Orissa to flow into the Bay of Bengal. The Kanha-Kisli jungles, of which we have had a glimpse earlier during Deva-Pitta's posting in Jabalpur, were the southern extent of the same almost continuous stretch of Sal jungle covering the watershed.

At Mandla we were admitted in the Government High School, which was located on the bank of the river. The river as it flowed past Mandla had plenty of clean and deep water in it. Further down-stream of the School, an aloof Englishman, the

Deputy Commissioner, lived by himself in the bungalow located on the river bank. Stone steps, next to the DC's Bungalow, led down to the river's edge from which some of us school boys took to swimming across the wide river. Later, after a monsoon flood, I once saw some villagers carry a 6-foot-long crocodile they had killed after it got trapped in the overflow of the River. It had a sobering effect on us who had been swimming in the river before that.

By early 1946, we had settled to a routine of often accompanying our father on some of his tours within the district. By then, the T- Model Ford car, which had succeeded the Austin- Seven, had been replaced with a Ford V-8 two-door sedan, a then more up-to-date model, purchased from an Ordinance Corps officer posted at Jabalpur. It was a comfortable and well-sprung vehicle, but with lesser road clearance and nala fording capability, as we were to discover later, as compared to the earlier T-Model.

On one of the early outings, while driving along a forest road through some fairly dense jungle, Deva-Pitta noticed some vultures circling above and then descending down amongst the trees in a patch of jungle adjacent to the road. An almost sure sign of a natural kill by a tiger or panther. Curiosity aroused, Father decided to investigate. Father with the loaded rifle led and the accompanying peon carried the shotgun as a backup. I followed a couple of paces behind. We had proceeded some distance and I could see Father getting uneasy on seeing that the vultures were keeping to their treetops. It was obvious that it was not prudent to proceed further, as the indications were that the predator was still close to the kill. We cautiously stopped and made our way back. I was now in the lead and after covering some distance stumbled upon a fledging Tree Pie chick. The chick had somehow fallen out of his nest. I picked up the young bird and brought him home. We named him 'Sher-Khan', based on Kipling's famous 'Jungle Book'.

MANDLA — 1946

Sadly 'Sher-Khan', the Tree Pie, did not live long enough as we could not feed him the right diet. He had grown quite friendly with the family dogs and seemed to recognize me when getting home from school on a bicycle. All his feathers were just shedding the sheaths they were enclosed in. It was a heartbreak losing the growing bird just when he was becoming very interesting. The name 'Sher Khan' resurfaced in later life when a Golden Labrador with that name stole the extended families affection over his lifetime.

*****

Sometime later, in another episode the family attempted a trip to Kanha-Kisli in the V-8 Ford. Father opted to adopt an unusual and risk-prone route to the sanctuary. We had been cautioned by the Forest Department people that the road we proposed using scarcely had any traffic on it and involved the car fording several nalas enroute. The forest road being taken by us generally followed the right bank of the Halon River, a prominent tributary that drained into the Narmada from the Kanha-Kisli area. Consequently, every now and then the road had to cross a succession of such nalas draining into the Halon. Later, we learnt from father that the forest department staff had indeed warned him that this route involved crossing one or two substantial nalas which had fairly wide and deep stretches of water that could be difficult to negotiate for the car. It was perhaps a shorter route to get us to our destination, so Father decided to take the chance

We had left the last village some ten miles behind and had been driving along in the thickly forested area, when we got to one of the problem nalas. The road descended sharply down to a stretch of about forty yards of water of uncertain depth. The road on the far side also sloped up steeply before it led away. As we held our breath, the V-8 Ford plunged into the water with a bit of a splash and managed to get about halfway across. The car slowed, floundered and

eventually just stalled. The engine just would not start thereafter. In later years one had learnt how it was important that the 'distributor' does not get flooded when fording such streams. We were stuck in the middle of a deep stretch of water and the car battery could not take the repeated efforts at starting the vehicle. It petered out after making some grumbling sounds.

As the water seeped-in, flooding the floorboard and began wetting our feet. There was complete silence for some time. Short tempers did not help, and woe betide anyone who tried to chip in with, "I told you so". It gradually dawned on us that it being fairly late in the afternoon, we would have to pass the night in the marooned car.

The stretch of the water where we were stuck had large shady trees on both sides which provided a canopy of greenery overhead enclosing us in complete darkness as night set in. A peacock called at dusk towards the Halon River with the full-throated 'mehaun-mehaun' roosting call. The jungle seemed to grow very quiet, with the tree frogs setting up a low 'beep-beep' chorus around us. We were wet and uncomfortable, but tried to settle down for the night. Our mother and the two sisters were on the rear seat, trying to keep their feet dry. Father and the two of us brothers huddled on the common front seat with our knees drawn up to keep our feet dry.

Soon the darkness engulfed us and we fell silent. We were all tense and tired with the unexpected turn of events, and beginning to doze off. The sound of the gentle lapping

of the water around us, coming through, the half-open side windows, lulled us into a state of stupor. After about an hour or so of complete silence within the car, Father suddenly stiffened alert and whispered that a large animal had come down the farther sloping road and was wading through the water towards us. On seeing the marooned car the animal stopped and after backtracking some distance, crossed the stretch of water somewhat upstream. Father's sharp hearing could follow the happenings clearly. We brothers were quite breathless ourselves trying to visualize what was happening. Despite the near total darkness that enveloped us, Deva-Pitta's acute hearing could even detect the heavy breathing of the animal going past us in the night.

Early next morning Father found where the previous night's 'heavy animal' had crossed over. The clear pug marks in the black wet clay showed that it had been a very large male tiger. The clear round huge pug marks had been left by the animal that had waded past us the previous night. We learnt that day how to differentiate between a male and a female's pug marks.

*****

On another tour trip in the V-8 Ford, we were a few miles short of our days destination , the Forest Rest House at Shahpura. Usually on this stretch of the dusty gravel road, we would often come across some Red Jungle Fowl scratching on the roadsides. We were all on the lookout for the possible birds, for the evening timings were just right. We were passing a series of open glades and grassy meadows in between clusters of Sal. It was about five in the afternoon with the sunlight at its best, lighting up the yellow and golden grass.

When I exclaimed "Tiger!" In an excited voice, no one seemed to believe me or even take note. Deva-Pitta just continued driving the car without pause. I had to emphatically insist that I had seen

a tiger sitting in the grass in the glade we had just past. At last something in my voice must have carried conviction as Father braked and stopped the car which had been coasting along at a fair speed. As the dust raised by the car enveloped and blinded us for some minutes, the car was reversed slowly whilst the dust settled down to about where I had initially reported the sighting, I pointed out the clear outline shape of a tiger's head as he sat motionless in the yellow grass about 200 yards away. "It's probably a stump of a tree which looks like a tiger's head"- someone remarked, as it seemed odd to everyone that at such an hour a tiger should be sitting around like this.

I insisted that I had clearly seen the tiger flick his ear, when I was looking at the "stump" when the car had sped by. No one seemed to believe me until almost on cue the tiger in the grass not only flicked his ears again, but also moved his tail so that everyone saw it. There was a scramble to pull out the rifle from its canvas case and get the cartridges out. It was least expected that the rifle would be required like this at such short notice. All this time the tiger kept sitting, looking fixedly away from us. We later found that the tiger's location in the grass was at a vantage point that allowed him a grandstand view of the village cattle that was ambling along the lower ground on the far side homeward bound in the late afternoon. This lower ground on the far side was defiladed from view from the road for us. A straggler may have strayed behind and given the tiger the chance he was looking for to make a kill.

It was a difficult head shot to take from about 200 yards and must have just missed. At the shot, the tiger jumped up and leapt full length across a hidden dry nala next to where he had been sitting. He then hurriedly galloped away and disappeared into the jungle beyond. We all got a full view of the tiger for those few seconds, with the sun's rays at a slant at that hour, lighting up the scene beautifully. It was an unforgettable event for us all.

THE LEOPARD ACROSS THE NARBADA

There was a cow killed by a large leopard in a very impoverished little hamlet on the far bank of the Narbada River. I accompanied Father in the effort to shoot this leopard as it was during the summer break from school. I however, have no recollection of how we crossed the river. Downstream of Mandla, there were places where the river had several clusters and groups of black lava rocks jutting out from the river, which enabled us to almost get across dry shod. A few odd thatch huts of the hamlet were located close to the river's edge, from where the ground sloped upwards gently over a distance to the edge of the mixed forest. The open ground had some sparse, short, green grass that the cattle could graze on.

Some shallow ravines cut across the grassy plain, along which the rain water ran off towards the river. A few trees were scattered here and there along the main ravines between the jungle and the huts. A machan had been put up in one of these trees. The machan was in the lower ground in a wide dry nala bed . The kill, the dead cow's bloated carcass, was about 25 yards from the machan and, owing to the configuration of the terrain, was on the same level as us. The machan thus did not overlook the kill, and what we only later realized was that the leopard may use the 'dead' space behind the bloated kill to play hide and seek with us after dark.

It was a black and brown colored full-grown cow that had been boldly killed by the leopard the previous night near the hamlet.

Being a fairly heavy animal for the leopard to carry away, he tried dragging it but dropped it after a distance as the thoroughly aroused village raised a hue and cry with the village dogs joining in the noise. It had later returned to the kill and eaten a portion in the usual manner of leopards by starting at the stomach at the anal end. The kill was left lying in the open, adjacent to a cluster of trees, one of which could take a well concealed machan. The kill had been covered over with leaves by the villagers to deter the vultures from getting to the carcass. Vultures would have finished it off in a short time if they had got to the dead cow. However, the summer heat had led to the dead cow being bloated and beginning to get smelly.

As dusk settled down, we could hear the people in the huts preparing for the evening meal. A thin film of smoke seemed to wrap the few flimsy huts. The noise of children being called by mothers and the sound of cattle being secured for the night, could be clearly heard by us on the machan. The sound of the gently flowing river beyond the hamlet also wafted across to us as the evening air cooled. Being in between the habitation and the mixed jungle we somewhat missed the birdsong and other noises that has a fascinating effect on the listener when sitting up.

Father had decided to use the trusted old 12-bore shotgun in dealing with the leopard, using buck-shot (LG-or Large Grape) in both the barrels. Though the . 405 Winchester rifle was handy, he seemed to prefer the shotgun as we were close to human habitation and a rifle shot could lead to unforeseen accidents. Since the use of a shotgun involved the three-cell torch light being operated separately to light up the target with the focused spotlight, I had to perform this vital task when the time came for this. To enable me to do this effectively, I had to sit a little behind to flash the light over Father's right shoulder. Unlike in the use of a rifle, a torch could not be clamped on onto a shotgun. We practiced this out

whilst it was still day light, to enable me to perform the supporting role without unnecessary movement.

The leopard, as expected, waited for the noises in the nearby huts to die down before coming to the kill. He came boldly, making no effort to conceal his move as we could hear the loud noise of his moving in the dry leaves as he came along. Besides this, we could easily follow his move from the almost continuous loud alarm calls as a series of loud "pheau", uttered by jackals that seemed to follow the panther, keeping it in sight. There seemed to be several jackals that were giving out this unusual alarm call repeatedly. It was a bit like a jungle 'marriage procession'. Father later recollected that he had first heard this same alarm call of a jackal while sitting up waiting for the Jhilpa Man-eater many years before. At that time he was not sure of it being a jackal's alarm call. It is a very loud and distinctive alarm call, quite unlike the usual wailing call described by some ungenerously as 'dead Hindu –dead Hindu', heard frequently near human habitation.

Whilst the jackals kept up the chorus of loud 'pheaus' around, the leopard arrived on the kill and shortly thereafter we could hear him beginning to eat noisily. With bated breath we got ready as rehearsed. When Deva-Pitta was ready, I pressed the torch button and the bright focused beam lit up the bloated cow. For a fraction of a second nothing happened, followed by a brief glint of the leopard's shining eyes before he bolted off to a flank. Only a blurred yellow streak was seen by us. It was too fleeting a target for Father to take a shot. I switched off the torch on Father telling me to do so and quietly resumed the vigil silently. Soon the chorus of jackals were at it again. The clever leopard was using the bloated cow to advantage, as the machan did not allow us to look beyond the kill and the dark shadow cast by it. This happened about three times, until Father engaged the 'yellow blurred streak' as the leopard seemed to be having the last laugh at our growing discomfiture.

The leopard seemed to be hit for in the raised dust cloud it seemed so , but nothing could be claimed with certainty. The second barrel had been emptied out by Father in the general direction of the disappearing animal. The torch beam was wildly moving to and fro, but the leopard seemed to have vanished into thin air. Thereafter, about half an hour or so later, we heard the distinct sound of the leopard grumbling with pain. Obviously, there were slight folds and undulations in the ground, which we could not discern by torchlight. The hurt leopard had taken cover in one such fold, so we decided to tackle the problem the next morning.

The next morning when we got to the area, there were some village cattle browsing around unconcerned at the previous night's happenings. Vultures had already gorged themselves on the leftover kill. Nobody seemed aware or worried about a wounded leopard in the area. The boy tending the cattle, unwittingly drifted close to where the wounded leopard was lying in a shallow drain. The leopard rose up with an angry snarl above the ground level, taking a wild swipe with his slashing claws. The boy tending the cattle leapt away, just evading being mauled. We could see the leopard's yellow canine teeth, as he let of blood curdling growls, one after the other. The previous night's shot had fortuitously broken his hip or else we would have been in some trouble. His fiery yellow hateful eyes, remained defiant to the end. The boy grazing the cattle had been very lucky that he had escaped unhurt. A wounded leopard is a most dangerous animal and must be put out of his misery soonest.

*****

THE TIMNI TIGER

The hamlet across the Narabada, where the leopard was shot in the last story, was on the left bank where the ground gradually sloped away from the main river. The edge of the mixed jungle was several hundred yards away. During the monsoon floods the water spilt over mainly on that side. The hamlet probably just a temporary cattle station, moved away to higher ground during the monsoons. However, conversely on the opposite or right bank the ground rose abruptly from the edge of the river bed some twenty five feet high or so. This riverbank cliff was covered by fairly thick, mixed jungle right up to the very edge. The three or four mile wide belt along the river was cut up by several ravines and nalas. The ground was undulating and had abundant grass for cattle to graze. Timni, was a small village about six miles from the district Headquarter town of Mandla and was located on the main road coming from Jabalpur to Mandla. This road's alignment generally followed the right bank of the river, separated by the three or four mile wide belt of mixed jungle. The staggered small villages like Timni along the road had large collection of milch cattle, including a large proportion of buffalos. Milk was supplied and sold in the town of nearby district town of Mandla.

The belt of mixed jungle between the road and the river, as brought out, was cut up by ravines and nalas . These watercourses cut fissures through the high bank, draining into the river during the monsoon, but thereafter remaining dry yet full of thick bushes and shady cover. The terrain thus was ideal for predators like tigers and leopards that could adapt themselves to cattlelifting, there being hardly any other wildlife prey except perhaps wild boars in such jungle. The plentiful grass attracted the cattle into the ravines and the cattle lifting predators thrived on these conditions. The terrain and the general setting, including the proximity of the river, may be kept in mind, as the story of the Timni Tiger unfolds. Cattle lifting tigers grow to be very strong and large, as compared to the deep jungle dwellers.

It was the last week of May 1946, on a very hot afternoon, that Deva-Pitta came back from the Courts with the news that he was going to sit up later that evening for a tiger that had killed a large milch buffalo near Timni village. The buffalo that was killed was to calve shortly, so the owner was even more aggrieved with his loss. I was as excited as could be when told that I could accompany Father for the venture. This was not too long after the leopard episode narrated earlier. I was eleven years old at that time, and very keen to share in any jungle adventure.

We drove to Timni in the V-8 Ford, and leaving the road got closer to the site of the kill along a rough cart track. We left the car at an open spot from where we walked about a mile and a half to the site of the kill with the guides and local shikaris. The tiger had a meal on the she-buffalo the previous night. The kill lay wedged in a depression next to a dry, flat clay patch in the bed of a dry nala. The nala was otherwise full of thick bushes and foliage and curved away sharply upstream from where the dead buffalo lay. The nala had cut its way through the cliff bank to flow into the main river stream, which was a short distance downstream from where the kill lay. It was getting late, so there was a quick look around before we climbed into the machan.

The machan had been put up in a stout Sal tree growing in the bed of the nala on a side halfway up the high side of the cutting. Once we climbed onto the machan, we were left there by our

local guides and shikaris. While settling down a little later, Father observed that should the tiger initially come along the cliff side jungle to take a preliminary look down at the kill, we would be at the same level as him. We were very uncomfortably close to the edge of the cutting. It was, however, too late to do anything about it. All we could think of was the necessity to remain completely still and hope to remain undetected. It was an uneasy thought and one had to keep hoping that the tiger would just not discover us in the machan. We hoped that after dark, in the bright moonlit night, we would remain in the shadow of the trees foliage around the machan.

The blistering hot day gave way to a pleasant cool breeze coming from the river, stirring the leaves gently around us. The jungle had a brooding silence, as there were no alarm calls or even the other bird songs that evening. Just as dusk was setting in there was a loud and sudden sound that Father identified as a tiger's call. It was not from too far away, but otherwise I cannot now describe the sound or even its direction. It was made probably to drive away the human intruders from the proximity of the kill. Soon it was night and after some time the bright moonlight flooded the place with dark shadows and patches of diffused moon light. We heard a bat soaring through the air as it flew down to the river, possibly to quench its thirst.

Without any warning there was the sudden sound of a heavy animal having jumped down onto the flat clay bed of the nala beneath and behind us. The tiger had arrived silently along the high bank of the river next to us but luckily, had decided to get down into the nala to approach the kill. It was around 9:00 PM and the bright moon was overhead. Looking down over the shoulder, we could see a large animal unhurriedly approaching the kill. It looked uniformly grey in the moon light. Father and I sat motionless, holding our breath. We could clearly hear the sound of the animal's breathing, as he seemed to be looking down at the

dead buffalo, wedged below him next to the mud bank on which he was standing. Then, abruptly, the tiger ploughed through the dense bushes on the far side and just left us wondering as to what had happened.

Father was quite perplexed as to what was happening, and I could sense his thoughts as he looked askance at me. What could have provoked the tiger to leave so suddenly ? I had sat motionless throughout, but Father seemed to think that maybe I had done something that had perhaps disturbed the tiger during those tense minutes. I had to silently suffer Father's annoyance and suspicion.

To further compound the situation, after some more time had elapsed, I whispered to Father that I just had to pass urine. Summer does require greater intake of drinking water owing to the greater perspiration to keep the body cool during the heat of the day. That evening it was different as it was getting pleasantly cool owing to the proximity of the river and so the water intake had to find the other way out. I could feel Father's wrath and regret having an eleven year old child on hand. Well, there was nothing we could do, so I was given a go ahead but to minimize the noise on the leaves below – was told in a whisper to aim the stream onto a thick branch to reduce the resultant noise. Inspite of my trying, I am afraid the noise it made on the dry leaves below our machan seemed loud enough to me, to be heard even in Mandla . It seemed to be the end of the tiger shooting adventures for me.

Perhaps the anticlimax and disappointment finally got me feeling suddenly drowsy with sleep. Father let me stretch out comfortably while he prepared himself to continue the vigil. He had not given up the hope that the tiger would come to the kill later during the night. I was soon fast asleep and probably dreaming of tigers, when around midnight, I woke up suddenly on the firing of the rifle by Father. I heard the noise of the rifle being reloaded and fired yet again.

The tiger had returned to the kill just before midnight and approached the dead buffalo from the other side. He was thus facing towards us now, but was squatting in such a manner that he presented a foreshortened and smaller target. The clay bank wedged the kill awkwardly, and when Father had switched on the light to illuminate the target, the tiger did not seem to notice and continued to eat. In the bright moonlight the tiger initially did not react to the torch light focused on him. At the shot being fired, the tiger flung himself full length backwards into the foliage of the nearby bushes. The second shot was fired roughly where Father thought he was. I was fully awake now, but never glimpsed anything of the tiger . However, I saw the agitation caused by the tiger, tearing wildly at the bushes and making the most blood curdling sounds. The gnashing and loud chattering of his teeth in agony on receiving the injury was a most frightening thing to witness.

The next several hours, intermittently the wounded tiger continued his agonising tearing and agitating the foliage. Gradually

there were silent spells, but the teeth grinding would resume time and again. By this time the wounded animal seemed aware of our location on the machan as we were using the torch frequently. We, however, never got to see anything of him. At daybreak the visibility improved and before the locals and the Shikaris arrived, Father thought that by firing a 12-bore birdshot into the bushes in the vicinity where the tiger had been through the night, may shift him so to make himself visible to enable Father to take a shot. Father asked me to fire this shot. It was the first shot I ever fired with a shotgun.

At the shotgun's scattered pellets peppering the bushes, nothing happened except the agitation in the bushes ceased and apparently the tiger moved away unseen by us. When we later descended from the machan and carefully took a look at the area where the wounded animal had vented his anger all night, we found a three inch bone splinter, a piece from the tiger's shattered thigh bone.

The tiger had just ahead of us, crossed the nala bed and ascended the steep slope on the far side, as the blood trail showed. The very fresh blood trail led straight up the side of an adjacent spur. The effort to move him with the shotgun shot had led to his trying to get away from the bushes where he had spent several hours in great pain. He managed to pull himself up the fairly steep slope, but still kept out of sight from the machan. The slope he had gone up, was too steep to follow the blood trail directly.

It was a tense situation as everyone knew that the tiger might at any time burst upon us from above while we were still in the lower ground of the nala bed. It was prudent to quickly and silently move away further upstream of the nala to where it curved round the lower end of the spur which the tiger had climbed.

Father realized it was not prudent having me around with him under the circumstances, so one of the local guides took me away

to a safe flank. I watched the proceedings from a safe flank. I could see Father's small group cautiously climbing from a flank along the spine of the spur up which the Tiger had climbed to cross over. Father, with the cocked rifle in hand at the ready, assisted by about two others, climbed slowly, warily, taking a few steps at a time.

The tiger had pulled himself up directly and straight up the top of the adjacent spur. By side-stepping some distance up along the nala, the spur could be climbed along a more gradual gradiant from a flank. This approach enabled Father to see both sides of the spur and also where the tiger seemed to be heading. Keeping roughly to the centre of the spur, they soon came across some fresh blood of the tiger where he had crossed over the spur at right angle to their approach. The very fresh blood trail now further led down a gradual slope into a shallow ravine, on the far side of which the wounded tiger was slowly climbing the slightly sloping ground on the far side.

As Father looked up in the direction taken by the wounded tiger, he saw the animal whip around and emitting a loud angry roar, charge towards them. The tiger was some forty yards or so from him when he began his angry assault. There was only some intervening light scrub through which he charged down the slight slope he had just climbed.

The second successive hit from the rifle stopped the great beast in his stride and he slid to a position, as if in repose, under a *renee* thorn bush. Even then he still seemed to hold his head up, and as we watched, with dignity let it slowly sink down into death. The fire in his bright yellow eyes faded out slowly in death.

Inspite of his shattered hind leg, the tiger had pulled himself up the steep slope and a little later charged headlong. He had obviously pulled himself up the slope using his very strong forelegs. During his headlong attack, Father did not notice the tiger being hamstrung by the shattered leg. However, the broken limb

must have impeded the valiant and brave animal in his desperate attempt to get at his tormentor.

He was an oversized male, with a round, fulsome fringe around his face. He must have weighed a great deal as we needed almost ten men to lift and carry him to the car.

* * * * *

As the party carrying the dead tiger wended its way towards where the car was left the previous day, I was leading with the guide, keeping some paces ahead, proudly carrying Father's now unloaded and empty .405 Winchester Rifle on my shoulder. We descended somewhat to cross a dry nala to get to the car, using the track that passed through a cutting. Imagine our shock and utter surprise as we got to the cutting to see another tiger turn hurriedly around and move quickly ahead of us until it disappeared from view. This second tiger had been coming down the track from the opposite direction and had turned around on seeing us. This surprise sighting goes to show how cattlelifting attracted these predators into this belt of mixed ravine and broken ground adjacent to the Narbada River.

* * * * *

The Timni Tiger's magnificent head was mounted on a black wooden shield by Van Ingen & Van Ingen's at Mysore. These taxidermists brothers, had done an excellent job of giving the tiger a somewhat off centre look, with a questioning and somewhat startled expression on his face – with his mouth slightly ajar. Deva-Pitta preferred this to the usual snarling face of the tiger.

This tiger became and remained the central trophy in our parental home, whereever it was, as 'home' moved from place to place, wherever Father's civil servant's job took him. The Timni

Tiger remained an icon of majestic beauty reminding us of those momentous days at Mandla in the period just before India gained Independence.

After the Jhilpa leopard's earlier episodes at Nagpur in 1943, the The Timni Tiger remained the next much talked of shikar event of the period. I had been with Deva-Pitta on both these occassions as a growing child. But having talked of these again and again in later years, memories have been repeatedly brushed up and kept freshened.

Deva-Pitta, our father, in later years settled down in Clement Town in Dehradun after retiring from service from Ujjain in Madhya Pradesh. He had started from Central Province, moved to Hyderabad during the Police Action, from where he moved for an extended tenure in Bombay (Mumbai), before returning to the reconstituted Madhya Pradesh before superannuating.

The Timni Tiger had faded over the years in his coloring – but his glass eyes still preserved the fire of yore – as he looked down from his perch. At Dehradun, shortly before he died on Baisakhi Day in 1995, Deva-Pitta turned to us brothers in reminiscencing while looking up at the magnificent but now faded head of The Timni Tiger, and said—" I felt a wave of remorse when he put his great head down as life ebbed out of him. The dignity with which I saw the light fade out of his brave face and eyes moved and saddened me."

SCHOOL AT NAINITAL

Nainital seemed a long distance away from backward and 'jungli' Mandla; our parent's home station then. We had earlier travelled to the north with the family for our holiday during the summer of 1942. So going away north from home was no big deal for us. We had spent nearly four months in Kashmir in 1942, but things were different now in July 1947, as both of us brothers were going to be in a boarding school, away from home for several months, until mid-December. Our school's winter closure would next bring us home for the three and a half months winter vacation as the school had no summer break, being a hill station.

Most significantly the country was attaining independence on 15 August. There were great expectations, and excitement yet some uncertainty and tension in the air. However, we were quite thrilled and excited with the change of being in Nainital; blissfully unaware, at that time, of what lay ahead.

Looking back now with hindsight, it was significant that the school was starting anew. The school campus had earlier been developed over the years since 1877, as a residential public school, meant for European children. With India attaining freedom, It was now to become an 'Indian' managed and staffed public School in an environment hitherto used, mainly for the Europeans. There was thus, some uncertainty and challenge in joining the school being set up at Nainital by the Birla Education Trust. 'Birla Vidyamandir' (BVM), as the school was named, was to now start as a completely new school, with Indian management and staff on 17 July 1947, in the existing estate of 62 acres, located just below the 'Sher-ka-Danda' height, on the eastern hill top overlooking the Nainital lake. The general altitude of the estate was almost 8000 feet above sea level.

School at Nanital – from Cheena Top

The predecessor schools under European Management had been 'Oak Openings School' (1877-1905); 'Philander Smith College' (1905-1941) and then during the Second World War, 'Hallet War School'(1941-1944). The school buildings and other facilities were already in existence with elaborate tin-shed covered paths interconnecting different parts of the school and hostel buildings. With the backdrop of the country's forthcoming independence, there were very high expectations, with the greatly aroused national patriotic fervour. The teaching staff and all of us were quite fired up with the opportunity and challenges involved.

We were surrounded by thick jungle and greenery, and in comparative terms isolated from the rest of Nainital. The school

was frequently visited by prominent national leaders. Pandit Nehru accompanied by Lady Mountbatten, agmonst others, visited the school within the first year. Lady Mountbatten wearing jodhpuri breeches, had ridden up on horse back along with Nehru. She lay down full length on one of the beds in our dormitory, light heartedly testing the bed for its comfort. Later, India's first Indian Commander –in- Chief General K M Cariappa also visited.

For Vijay, my younger brother and I, the jungle around us with the bird and wildlife activity around our school area, quite attracted us. We quickly adapted to the routine activities of the school, in both work and play. Evening assembly consisted of the singing of some simple prayer songs and bhajans which was often with a most beautiful backdrop of a crimson sunset in the west. The Camel's Back feature *(Deopatta 7,991 feet high)* on the far side of the lake, and adjacent to Nainital's highest peak, *Cheena (8,569 feet high)* silhouetted sharply against the horizon. Behind us on the grass slopes of Sher-Ka-Danda, we would often see gorals in the evening sunlight. Sometimes, but rarely, the drifting breeze would carry the sound of a barking deer from the jungle covered deep ravine behind our hostel, warning of the presence of a leopard. In the afternoons the large bearded Lammagieire vulture would fly, gliding along the contour searching the slopes of the heights towards Ladhya- Kanta. We mistakenly initially thought the Lammagieire was a Golden Eagle. With a wing span of almost eight feet, it was a conspicuous lonely flier of the himalayan hills.

Our winter break of 47'-48' was spent at our Father's next station of Narsinghpur. It was an independent subdivision and for Father, was considered a step towards getting a full fledged district as a 'deputy commissioner'. More than a hundred years before, Major General Sleeman had been posted here as the 'DC' in his effort to eradicate the 'thuggee' menace.

We were on the tennis court at the Narsinghpur Club on 30th January evening when the news of Mahatma Gandhi's assassination came in. A pall of gloom seemed to set in on receipt of the shocking news.

At a prayer meeting organized at Narsinghpur, our mother sang a beautiful baneful Surdas song: *'deenan dukh haran dev – santan hitakari--------'*.

The bungalow at Narsinghpur had a large patch of scrub jungle adjacent to it. A nala with clean flowing water flowed through it, and we brothers spent happy hours exploring the varied birdlife in it. There was a family of otters that we discovered living in the nala, who were a delight to watch, gamboling about in the water. We would spend much time observing them from a hidden vantage point.

HYDERABAD—POLICE ACTION 1948

By September 1948, the events of the 'Police Action' in Hyderabad led to Deva-Pitta being assigned the task of going in as 'Civil Administrator' or 'Collector', of Adilabad District. It was during our next winter break from school that we joined the parents at Adilabad. It was the most under-developed district of the erstwhile state of Hyderabad. A minor military operation had been mounted over the Paingunga River bridge involving a locomotive and some open wagons from Balarshah across the border. There was hardly any resistance by the Hyderabad forces or Razakars.

When we got home to join our parents at Adilabad, we found them occupying a Forest Rangers accommodation as a stop gap arrangement. The district officers' bungalows were not constructed till then. There was still a small contingent of Gorkha troops at Adilabad who were in the process of moving back to their unit. There was also a grass airstrip at Adilabad that had been bombed by Indian Air Force 'Liberator' bombers during the operations. However, by the time we got there in mid-December the craters had been filled up. We would gleefully take turns at learning to drive in jeeps on the airstrip. It was fun driving on the obstacle free strip. There were about three well used World War II jeeps assigned for Father's work.

Some time later we even had a distinguished visitor, Brigadier S D Verma from Hyderabad for a brief visit on behalf of Major

General J N Choudhary, the Military Governor. He landed on the airstrip in a 'Devon' twin engine aircraft. Our mother presented the visitor a bunch of pink lotuses at the airfield. The aircraft had the formation sign of the Armoured Division – a black elephant on a yellow background – painted on the fuselage on its nose.

Beyond the airstrip was a vast area covered by scrub jungle. Brother Vijay and I along with Nawab, our black mixed-breed retriever, were once just loitering in this area, where occasionally we would flush the odd hare for Nawab to give chase. On this occasion, fortunately, I had the dog chained as we ambled around the area. At one place Nawab strained at the chain trying to sniff at something in the dry leaves under some bushes. Just in time I yanked him away as only a couple of inches away from his nose was the head of a large Russel's Viper lying concealed with his camouflaged coloring. The snake gave us a malevolent look with his beady, unblinking eyes before he slithered away. He was as thick as a man's arm and had the prominent triangular head of a viper. We had a frightening experience and it was lucky that I had Nawab on a chain and chanced to see the snake just in time before he attacked the dog.

There was an abnormally high number of carnivorous animals in the jungles of the erstwhile princely state. Both tigers and leopards had taken to cattlelifting as during the period before the Police Action they had destroyed most of the deer and nilgai in the widespread jungle. Being Muslims, wild boars were, however, left alone. Being largely armed with muzzle-loading muskets, the Razakars avoided tackling tigers and leopards. Owing to this the sighting of leopards and tigers was fairly frequent beside the main roads as they seemed to follow the cattle coming home in the evenings.

Once Father, returning from a tour in a jeep, absentmindedly drove past a 'red cow' in the late afternoon, belatedly realising that it had been a tiger that had ambled across the road. This was

especially so over a stretch of road a few miles from the district headquarters, on the road leading towards the state capital . Some seven miles from Adilabad the road passed close to a water reservoir called Mawala. There were frequent sighting of a tiger or leopard by casual motorist on this particular stretch of the road near the reservoir. We would often carry out an evening drive in a jeep using a powerful spot-light.

One evening we came across a family of five tigers near Mawala. They were obviously a mother with four fully-grown cubs. It was a sight to see them in the glare of the spot light just lounging amongst some teak saplings. Father was away on some duty and Mr Prasan Dave was holding 'fort' in his absence. Dave was an ex-army officer, taken into the Indian Administrative Service. He was greatly admired by us brothers. That memorable day, to his credit, he left the family of tigers unmolested. A few days later, sadly, one of the district officers shot one of the cubs during a night drive.

Probably owing to the cattle lifting menace the man vs animal conflict led to stray incidents. A tigress with cubs mauled some villagers. Some time later a man was killed in the same area. Father decided to camp in the affected area. A suitable forest rest house was used at a place called Boath. All cattle kills made by carnivores were to be reported and efforts would be made by Father and Mr Dave to shoot the animal by sitting up over such kills. Mr Dave had been encouraged to partake in big game shooting by Father. He had acquired a . 375 Magnum rifle for the purpose and had already bagged a male leopard with it.

On the second day camp at Boath, news came in that there were two tiger kills and a leopard kill reported in widely spread area. The leopard kill was at a close by village and its news came in first in the morning. Deva-Pitta visited the kill with us brothers in tow and gave the villagers the instructions for setting up a suitable machan. The young calf that had been taken as the cattle

were coming back to the village the previous evening lay well concealed under some *karonda* bushes growing under a cluster of tall sal trees. The kill was covered up with some branches by the villagers to protect it from vultures and other scavengers during the day.

Later that morning, further news of the two tiger kills from other places also came in. It was then decided that while Father would sit up with brother Vijay over one of these kills, Mr Dave was to get to the second kill's site directly from Nirmal , his place of stay as the Subdivisional Officer of the area. Suitable machans had already been set up at the two sites by local shikaris deputed for the purpose. It thus fell to my lot to sit up on the leopard kill, chaperoned by David, Father's jeep driver. I was to use Fathers trusted old hammer shotgun, a weapon I had grown up with, and a spare shotgun was arranged for David. I was as excited as could be. As a thirteen-year-old I was raring to go. After seeing Father and brother Vijay drive off in the other jeep for sitting up on one of the tiger kills, David and I drove to the site of the leopard kill well before sundown.

David and I were comfortably settled in the machan well before the evening. We had the two shotguns and a spare torch for the task in hand. The jeep was parked some distance away and we were suitably organised for the evening. I had even practiced how to cock the shotgun noiselessly, and told David to let me first take a shot before he chipped in if required. I told him to sit quite still and not to make any movement during our vigil.

The village was about half a mile away The sound of children at play, dogs barking at the returning cattle, the muffled sound of wooden bells worn around their necks, and the dust mingling with the smoke of fires cooking the evening meal carried on the air. This setting has a timeless quality about it and has a beautiful expression in Hindi '*gau dhuli bela*'—"the hour of the dust stirred up by the cows"—to describe it all.

The machan faced roughly west, so as dusk descended and as the light began to slowly fade, the top of the tall sal in front of us under which the kill lay was silhouetted against the still bright sky. As evening was turning into dusk, a large horned owl alighted on the top branch of the sal tree and sent off a blood-curdling and very loud call that must have been heard upto a great distance. David and I were both quite startled by the sudden explosion of sound. As the owl departed from his perch I glanced down and saw the leopard emerge in the gloom near the kill. I took a shot quickly in the fading light.

The shotgun blast bowled the panther over, even as David was recovering from the loud sound emitted by the owl from the tree tops before it flew away.

It was all over and we got back to the rest house where my mother awaited our return. In later years she would recount how the thirteen-year-old had rushed in to announce his success.

(Note- Later, when I got more interested in 'Birds', I could identify the owl as a Forest Eagle-Owl [Buba nipalensis nipalensis] . The call it had emitted sounded like a –" diabolical blood-curdling shrieks as of a woman being strangled, which could well qualify it for the name 'Devil Bird.'- "Salim Ali")

Mr Dave had taken up his place on the machan made for the purpose and had taken a shot at a tigress after she started to feed on the kill well after dark. The tigress was wounded and got away. Next morning with Father in charge, we tried locating the stricken tigress. She growled menacingly at us a couple of times but moved away. Later, after a few days, Mr Dave came up with her after she had become very weak and had taken shelter in a nullah.

The third sit up with Father and brother Vijay was also productive. It was very clearly a tiger's kill but by chance a large leopard arrived after dark and started to feed on the kill. Father thought it was the tiger, and took the shot with his rifle after switching on the three-cell torch attached to the weapon. The

target was standing broadside on and the bullet had gone right through the leopard's chest, exiting on the far side. In the fleeting flash of a second or two neither Father nor Vijay could make out that it was not a tiger that had been fired at. The animal had bounded away after the shot. Next morning we found the large leopard dead some distance away. He had bled profusely from both flanks, the shot having gone through his chest. Later, we found that the leopard had a three-inch-long spike of a wild date palm embedded between the toes of one of his front paws. This must have affected his ability to hunt. This may possibly explain why he risked stealing a tigers kill.

When we returned to Nainital after the extended winter break, we carried the duly cleaned out skulls of the two leopards shot at Boath with us and presented these to the school's biology museum. Fifty years later they were still there when we got to visit the alma mater. The existing staff knew nothing of the past as to how these leopard skulls had got there.

NANDED—KAULASH – 1949-50

The next winter break from school took us to Deva-Pitta's new place of posting. He had been shifted laterally to Nanded and given the additional charge of Nizamabad district. Nanded is well known for having Sachkhand Guru Sahib Gurudwara, and is a pilgrimage place for the Sikhs from all over the country. Tenth Guru Govind Singh had been martyred here on the banks of the Godawari River.

That year, I was to prepare for my high school board examination in March- April 1950 and tried to concentrate on my preparations. Unlike Adilabad, there was no comparable jungle to distract our attention in this district, until quite by chance Father discovered Kaulash, a seemingly innocuous jungle patch through which the road leading to Hyderabad passed. This place was a couple of hours driving distance away from Nanded, and Father had quite ignored its existence until once while passing by, he had seen some vultures descending onto what seemed like a natural kill of a tiger. He could not stop on that occasion owing to some commitment, but he realised that the jungle held out promising possibilities.

There was a small rest house on the roadside in the area, which was located beside a deep nala, lined with tall white-trunked *Arjun* trees. Some distance away and only just visible from the motor road, were the ruins of an old fort, close to which nestled the main village of Kaulash. The Raja Sahib of Kaulash, resided in the village and was the main zamindar and feudal overlord of the area. The Kaulash fort ruins and its immediate surroundings were overgrown with mixed jungle, and closer to the village there were several large *Mahua* trees scattered around. The village itself was outside the jungle. The jungle stretched away broadly, but narrowed down considerably before the road to Hyderabad passed through it further to the east. When driving past towards Hyderabad, the jungle seemed only a narrow insignificant belt, and its potential for some shikar only discovered later.

The Raja Sahib of Kaulash proved most obliging and helpful. Once, Deva-Pita contrived a stop-over at the Kaulash Rest house on his way back from the state capital at Hyderabad. He and brother Vijay sat up on a machan over a live bait near where Father had once seen while transiting what seemed like a tiger's kill. Vijay saw the tiger in the defused moonlight, avoiding the bait and leaving it unmolested. The Raja Sahib who had helped making the impromptu arrangements, told Father later that it was a wily old beast, and must have seen the machan and its occupants.

The Raja Sahib later offered to help organise a few days shikar stay at the Kaulash Rest House for us. Father accepted the kind offer of the Raja Sahib's with the proviso that he would leave us brothers at the rest house with a cook for a few days, but made it clear that we were forbidden to try for the crafty old tiger until Father could be with us. He could only sparingly spend some time with us owing to the pressure of work having two districts to look after.

Meanwhile, Father had acquired for us a German Mauser 'Thirty Springfield' (30 -06) rifle in Hyderabad, and we brothers were raring to use it. As a special consideration, I was allowed a few days break from my preparation and studies. Father left us at Kaulash for some days in the care of the Raja Sahib and managed to get a most memorable character named 'Hyder Mian' as our

guide, chaperone and shikari. Hyder was a barely four and a half foot tall policeman, recruited exclusively for his prowess in shikar. He sported a muzzle loading musket taller than himself. When he would run out of percussion caps, he told us that he could improvise these from scraping the *'masala'* from safety matches and making these 'caps' himself. How the Raja Sahib or Father arranged for him is now impossible for me to recollect.

Hyder Mian would always proudly wore a discarded khaki riding corduroy breeches of a cavalry *sowar*. The breeches were meant to be laced around the wearer's knees with puttees wound over the riding boots. In Hyder's case, being very short, he let the untied laces flap around his ankle. He obviously wore these as full-length trousers as a prestige issue rather than their utility . He seemed to know the Kaulash jungles like the back of his hand.

Even as a fourteen-year-old, I was almost a foot taller than Hyder,but he quickly sized the two of us brothers up and took us in hand. On the first day, Hyder decided to take us to the Kaulash fort, as he said several sloth bears sought its shelter during the day.

We got to the entrance of the fort and took up a position overlooking the jungle path leading into it. Hyder insisted that the bears homed on to the Fort at sunrise and our vantage place was suitable to ambush them. After passively waiting out for about half an hour, I suggested to Hyder that to instead of waiting passively, we take a walk along the jungle track along which the bears were expected to come to the fort. With Hyder leading with his musket held horizontally on his shoulder, I was next with the Mauser rifle and brother Vijay followed, carrying the shotgun.

We had gone along the jungle track only a few hundred yards, when looking over Hyder's head I saw a sloth bear ambling across the track some fifty yards ahead of us. Hyder was looking down for pug marks in the dust on the track. By the time I drew his attention to the bear, it had crossed over the

track, and a second sloth bear closely followed the first. Both bears were ambling along with their heads slung low. They were moving slowly and had crossed the track obliquely and seemed quite unaware of us.

At my shot, the targeted second bear flung himself at the other and they got into an all out fight which lasted for a couple of minutes. Abruptly the shot animal collapsed, leaving the surviving animal looking puzzled and confused, before it rushed off into the jungle. I had reloaded the bolt action Mauser but withheld taking a second shot as it was not possible to tell which one had been fired at. Hyder Mian was delighted with the success.

That same afternoon, after attending to the skinning of the bear, Hyder quietly borrowed the shotgun and a couple of 'spherical' ball cartridges. He claimed he was going to 'shoot' some fish in the nearby nullah. I am afraid both Vijay and I did not quite realise what he was up to. The nala held plenty of dark green deep pools of water, but that it had large size fish in it, came as a big surprise for us. While we hung around the rest house after the morning's exertions and watched the skinning of the morning bag, Hyder had disappeared towards the nala. We later learnt that he had climbed onto an overhanging branch of one of the trees, and had secured the shotgun to the branch with a cord. He then sat quietly, with the gun ready, waiting for the big fish to rise to the surface as he knew it would.

Some time later we heard the loud 'bang' of the shotgun being discharged. Vijay and I dashed across to where we knew Hyder Mian was, and saw the most incredible sight of him struggling in the water with an enormous fish that he had shot. The head of the large fish, probably a *Mullee* or a *Maral* was quite smashed in and gory with blood. When we helped Hyder out of the water we realised that the fish was bigger in length than the shikari. He was having difficulty holding it up in the water. When the fish rises it lets off some bubbles before its head gets close to the surface.

That is when the shot strikes it from above. It was quite a surprise for us that such a large fish was there in the seemingly small nala.

*****

Hyder now switched his full attention to a large male leopard, whose pug marks he had shown us near the fort on the first day when we had shot the sloth bear. He had organised for us to sit up on a machan in one of the *Mahua* trees with a live goat bleating away to attract the leopard. The goat seemed aware of the exercise as after leaving us on the machan, Hyder had left us and moved away as the evening set in, the goat called or bleated a couple of times and then curled up comfortably to 'let things develop'. The goat seemed to know that we were keeping 'watch' in the *Mahua* tree. He was obviously a seasoned campaigner and knew the routine of being tied up like this.

Nothing happened thereafter, but after it got dark we heard a sloth bear climb the near by *Mahua* tree and, disconcertingly close to us, heard the unmistakable sound of his breaking a branch or two before loudly sucking the *Mahua* sap, making loud rasping noises. It was not a comfortable thought that ours was the next *Mahua* tree he was likely to address. Later on Hyder's arrival to take us down, the goat resumed his bleating, after the unsuccessful evening.

I kept wondering later, what we would have done if the bear had climbed our *Mahua* tree ?

The leopard, too, was obviously a seasoned campaigner, for we tried changing the machan site over the next few evening and even the bleating goat, but he seemed adept at locating us and avoiding being shot at. Several times over the next few days, he seemed to get the better of us. More than once the goat made such desperate sounds of being choked to find it only struggling with the rope he was tied with. On switching on of

NANDED—KAULASH – 1949-50

the torch light, the goat would look innocently into the beam of light, as if nothing was the matter. I suspected the leopard watching over these proceedings, remaining well concealed nearby. Hyder knew all about this particular animals behaviour and antics.

On one of those evenings when walking back after the failed sit up efforts, Hyder Mian told us that during the summer months the *Mahua* trees are abuzz with honey bees collecting nectar from the yellow-colored,fleshy flower and fruit of *Mahua*. A very potent brew is prepared by villagers from the fermentation of the *Mahua* fruit. In the wild, the ripe fruit litters the floor and the sugar rich fruit begins to ferment owing to the ambient heat. Sloth bears frequently imbibe plenty of this fallen fermenting fruit to get 'high'. Their pug marks meander along as they stumble around in a stupor. Hyder also mentioned that sloth bears are known to climb the wild date palm trees scattered around at the edge of the jungle to imbibe the '*toddy*' from the pots slung up by the villagers to collect the '*neera*'. This, too, begins to ferment. Sometimes an inebriated bear falls off the tall date palm, but usually suffers no injury from it.

Finally it was to be our last evening at Kaulash. Hyder suggested that we change track and try occupying a ground hide to possibly get a shot at some wild boar on this our last evening. It was a welcome change as the mosquitoes had driven us to despair sitting up for the leopard near the village.

We left the rest house well in time to get to where Hyder Mian had selected for our evenings effort. This place was at least a couple of miles away from the village, and well away from any habitation.

Hyder selected a spot where the jungle was thinning out with clumps of bushes scattered around. He swept the dry leaves aside and made a hide with leafy branches collected from nearby for concealment. The site selected covered a faintly discernable game

trail. The leafy branches concealed the three of us well enough as we sat down behind them on the ground.

We were soon settled, keeping the weapons handy and within easy reach, with minimum effort and movement to use these when required. Our concealment was soon tested as some time later, a peacock in full plumage came along the game trail, coming straight towards our hide before passing us by within just a few yards. The peacock, in full resplendent colour, at such close proximity was a dazzling sight in the fading light of the evening. Hyder Mian, the poacher in him fully aroused, was almost drooling at the sight of the magnificent bird as it passed by, pleading in whispers to let him shoot this prized shikar for himself. The peacock not detecting us was reassuring, as it is considered one of the most sharp-eyed bird in the Indian jungle.

About half a hour later, after the peacock had gone by and we had again settled quietly to our vigil, a large leopard walked straight towards our hide along the same game trail the bird had followed earlier. He was so close that I remember actually holding my breath for fear that he might hear my sudden intake of breath at his close proximity. One could see every detail of his face, through the thin screen of foliage concealing us. The loose fold of his skin under his chin swaying slightly as he began to wheel away to move past our hide.

He then seemed to pause slightly in his stride, looking away from our side on hearing some slight jungle sound. While he was looking away, it gave me the opportunity to quickly raise the Mauser and take a shot at his side as he began moving forward, away from us. He leapt into the air and fell awkwardly, snarling and biting at his far side where the bullet had exited. He bounded away, however, as I tried to get a second shot at him.

It was all quite sudden and in the failing light, Hyder quietly led us away along a safe route. It would seem that the same big leopard which had played hide and seek over several evenings

with us nearer the village, fell into an ambush we had laid for wild boar. It took us some time to get our wits about us at the sudden turn of events. We quietly walked back to the Rest House as darkness set in. I might confess in hindsight that we were all quite shaken up by the suddenness of the event.

Next morning when we got close to the previous evening's happenings, enroute we came across a couple of large wild boars, standing still and looking like black boulders. I am afraid I made a hash of the shot that I took with the Mauser from well over a hundred and fifty yards and missed clean. Perhaps the uncertain tension in the pit of one's stomach at getting to grips with a wounded leopard, contributed to the muffed shot. I was fourteen and Vijay twelve and inspite of Hyder Mian's jaunty confidence in us, we were feeling the pressure of the uncertain situation in hand. We were missing our Father's presence at such a time.

Fortunately, we found the leopard dead some distance away. The shot had shattered his liver. He was a beautiful specimen. As I have said before, a panther or leopard is quite the most beautiful and graceful of Indian wildlife.

The shikar sojourn at Kaulash turned out to be a most memorable one. In later years we would fondly remember our Shikari friend and companion Hyder Mian for all the adventures we shared with him. Every thing about him was quite remarkable. His short stature, his oversized blunder-buss or muzzle loading gun, made him a cartoonist's delight, but above all his cheerful enthusiasm and zest for Shikar were a treat to behold and share. I am sure he was the champion 'poacher' of the bygone Nizam's Hyderabad days. Recording these events more than sixty years later, I sometimes wonder if Hyder Mian will still be wearing his worn-out cavalry *sowar's* breeches as jauntily, while leading us to our next adventure as cheerily in the happy hunting grounds, were we must surely meet again, after our close association at Kaulash.

Nanded was otherwise an unattractive, over-crowded city. Here too there was no proper residential accommodation for the district's administrative staff. During January 1950, a ceremonial parade was held at which Deva-Pita took the salute and read out the preamble to the Indian Constitution, with the stirring words :- '*We, the people of India, give to ourselves ....*' It was a momentous occasion, but we as school boys hardly realised the historical significance of what was happening. Father wore a black *achkan* with *churidar* pyjamas and a white Gandhi cap while taking the salute at the parade, mainly of policemen and *gurudwara* guards.

STATE CAPITAL – HYDERABAD

By the time we came back from Nainital for the next winter's extended holiday, Father had been again elevated and moved to the then state capital of Hyderabad. He was appointed the Custodian of Evacuee Property for the state. A tricky task that he performed with scrupulous firmness and despatch. Sadly it moved us away from the outings in the Jungle.

During our next few winter holidays from school, we spent these at the state capital. The twin cities of Secunderabad and Hyderabad were a complete change for us. We moved house several times during Father's almost four years stay at Hyderabad, finally getting a spacious bungalow close to the Secunderabad Club. Each time we would come back from school for the winter break from Nainital, we would come to a different house. Last of these was on 'Sikh Road,' close to the race course and Mehboob College in Secundrabad.

Our spacious colonial-styled bungalow, with a large compound was directly under the flight path of the Indian Air Force Basic Flying Academy set up there at Begumpet. There was never a dull moment for us with a endless stream of 'Tiger-moth' biplanes and 'Harvard' trainer aircraft flying past hour after hour, almost every day, right over our place. Sometimes, odd ones of them would carry out what appeared to be a simulated emergency drill having the machine come floating down making coughing and sputtering noises and restarting just in time to regain speed and height. There was an open space and '***maidan***' just beyond our compound which was used thus . Luckily, we never saw a actual mishap take place. The 'Harvard' trainer aircraft were a particularly noisy affair. We could clearly see the pilot and co-pilot in the cockpit as they flew past in the training sorties.

Father had acquired a very spirited Golden Retriever puppy from a well known Hyderabad breeder, Colonel Sayeed, a retired officer of the Hyderabad Lancers. 'Toby' was the first of highly pedigreed pets that thereafter became a part of the family. A pup from the same litter had been presented to the Indian Prime Minister, Pandit Nehru, and had been named 'Madhu'. Colonel Sayeed was a polo playing horse cavalry officer with an aristocratic background. He in later years settled in Shimla, where I would meet him when posted at Sabathu with my Battalion in the Himachal Hills.

Toby grew into a very handsome and much loved pet of the family. As with all pets the head of the family received special attention. Deva-Pitta always received that preferential treatment from Toby, even as he jostled about in his rough play with us brothers, as he treated us as his equals. As he grew big and strong, he would quite wrestle with me, and I had to be watchful as his eyes would suddenly become serious and even menacing at times.

By this time, quite motivated to go into the defence services, I was preparing to try for the Joint Services Wing of the National Defence Academy, located at Dehradun. Being very poor in maths it took me more than a couple of attempts to qualify. A successful trip to the Selection Centre South at Bangalore followed, which got me to Dehradun sometime in July 1952. It was a reassuring feeling to get to Clement Town, itself half-tucked away in some beautiful looking sal forests . A lifelong bonding with the service was beginning with the feeling of youthful patriotic zeal to become a man amongst men in the service of the Motherland.

On the threshold of manhood, we were day and night put through the paces, and instilled with a value system based on camaraderie and a sense of commitment and honour. Most of us were from similar background, from families like my own. Some from public schools like The Doon School, or The RIMC (now renamed as Rashtriya Indian Military College), or Mayo College at Ajmer. I proudly was amongst the first to come from my school at Nainital. Later, many others including my younger brother Vijay were to follow. The trauma of partition still coloured the lives of many of our comrades.

NAINITAL – 1947-52

Here, I would like to pause in this narration of jungle stories and other events of one's boyhood years, and go back a little and dwell briefly on the grounding we got at our school in Nainital. My brother was nine and I was eleven when we had joined School in July of 1947, barely a month before the country attained freedom on 15 August 1947. It was a newly set up effort at having such a public school in a campus where hitherto only European children had schooled. The then school management and staff did an admirable job of blending the East-West ethos in those nascent years. These were impressionable years for us boys and the school became a home away from home for us.

Birla Vidyamandir (BVM) was located in the most attractive surroundings. It was in the midst of a fairly thick mixed jungle of oak , rhododendron, stunted *ringal* bamboo, nettle and several types of wild berries. The birds we learnt to recognise in those surroundings were the vocal Scimitar Warbler and the blue Himalayan Whistling Thrush, which would fleetingly 'whistle' past us in the misty surroundings. We could also identify several types of Tits moving about in the jungle in mixed flocks. A larger bird sometimes seen picking berries in the bramble was the conspicuous Himalayan yellow billed Blue Magpie. It was aptly called the *'lumb-putch'*(long tail) in the local language. It had a distinctive loud call. A cheeky bird, moving around in small flocks of up to three or four, essentially a fruit eating-bird but not averse to stealing other smaller birds eggs and unattended young chicks in their nests.

A copy of an early edition of Salim Ali's illustrated book on birds, had been gifted to elder sister Meera by Deva-Pita was purloined by us, which we brothers learnt to use in the mountain environment. We were soon branded as the *'cheedi-mar'* (Bird-hunters) brothers by our schoolmates. We even had a small collection of bird eggs between us. Vijay was particularly adept at 'skinning' birds that we had brought down with catapults or an air rifle which one of the boys had. One of brother Vijay's class-mates had a BSA .177 air rifle, which was a popular source of our adventuresome exploits.

During spring, the hills would resound to the melodious sound of the repetitive call of the 'Indian Cuckoo' (*Cuculus micropterus)*. It seemed as if the bird was announcing *'Kafal Paako.'* The hill folks believed that, the unseen bird told us of the ripening of the popular wild jungle berry much sought after by the Himalayan Black Bear. This melodious call of *'Kafal Paako'* was loud and audible over considerable distances, as is the summertime *'koel's'* repetitive calling in the plains. However, it had an enchanting resonance that echoed in the pine jungles and the mountain environment around Nainital.

The mountain top location of the school was such that it gave a wide view of the plains, towards the south and southwest, stretching right up to the blurred horizon, which merged with the distant curvature of the earth. Kathgodam and Haldwani in the south were barely visible as indistinct smoke covered smudges, at the foot of the hills. The Terai plains beyond faded away into shades of blue in the distant haze. Towards the east within the hills, but at much lower altitudes, were Bhim Tal, Naukucia Tal, and the Sat Tal cluster of smaller lakes. None of these, however, were actually visible from our school's location.

On the other side, on the northern end of the school's estate, tucked away in the oak forest on the flank of the Sher-Ka-Danda feature, was a spot we called "snow view". On a clear day, this view point gave us a breathtaking vista of the perennial snow covered range of peaks which stretched from west to east on the northern horizon. The snow covered range included Bandar-Pooch, Trishul, Kamet, Nanda-Devi and Nanda-Kot, fading away towards Nepal in the east. The vast visible area between us and the snow covered ranges, comprised the catchment area of India's most sacred rivers, Ganga and Jamuna. On a clear day the snow range seemed so close.

The intervening successive ridges and valleys in varying shades of grey and blue gave it all an ethereal setting with the backdrop of the towering snow-covered range behind. At sunrise the snow-covered range would emerge from the haze of predawn light with the morning sun's rays lighting up the peaks in hues of pink turning to gold. The beauty of that sunrise would last for a few moments and remains a unforgettable memory. It would be freezing cold to get up early enough to get to the viewpoint to witness the magic minutes.

Jim Corbett in the Introduction to his Book 'My India' describes the northern view from the top of Cheena, which was almost the same as was visible from our schools 'snow view', thus:

> *"Immediately below you is a deep well-wooded valley running down to the Kosi river. Beyond the river are a number of parallel ridges with villages dotted here and there; on one of these ridges is the town of Almora, and on another,the cantonment of Ranikhet. Beyond these again are more ridges, the highest of which, Dungar Buqual, rises to a height of 14,200 feet and is dwafed into insignificance by the mighty mass of the snow-clad Himalayas. Sixty miles due north of you, as the crow flies, is Trisul, and to east and to the west of this imposing 23,406-foot peak the snow mountains stretch in an unbroken line for many hundreds of miles".*

> *"Where the snows fade out of sight to the west of Trisul are first the Gangotri group, then the glaciers and mountains above the sacred shrines of Kedarnath and Badrinath, and then Kamet made famous by Smythe. To the east of Trisul, and set further back, you can just see the top of Nanda Devi (25,689 feet), ,the highest mountain in India. To your right front is Nanda Kot, the spotless pillow of the goddess Parvati, and a little farther east are the beautiful peaks of Panch Chuli, the 'five cooking-places' used by the Pandavas while on their way to Kailas in Tibet."*
>
> *"At the first approach of dawn, while Cheena and the intervening hills are still shrouded in the mantle of night, the snowy range changes from indigo blue to rose pink, as the sun touches the peaks nearest to heaven the pink gradually changes to dazzling white. During the day the mountains show up cold and white, each crest trailing a feather of powdered snow, and in the setting sun the scene may be painted pink, gold, or red according to the fancy of heaven's artist."*

The house masters and teachers of the newly set up school in a jungle-clad and somewhat isolated environment developed a flavour and ethos quite apart. The bonding and close friendships that we made in our stay at Nainital became a part of our lives thereafter. Most of these school time closenesses sustain to this day. The teachers were all addressed as '*Guru-jis.*'

Our exposure to our own culture, and classical and semi-classical music in the form of simple prayers in the form of bhajans was greatly fancied and liked by us all. Our music teacher, Mr. Apte,who was from Gwalior, had his room next to our dormitory. At the crack of dawn, he would begin practicing his singing by 'clearing his throat' in the early morning ragas in an effortless manner. As the sound of the '*tamboora*' wafted in, it created an enthralling ambience as we were all ears listening to the sound of music which seemed so apt for the early hours.

At mealtimes, a short Sanskrit 'grace' preceded the meal. Our Sanskrit teacher, Shri Narain Dutt Pande, had given the prayer its meaningful wordings. One of us would volunteer to recite the main stanzas in a loud voice, after which others would join in with the refrain of '*Om Shanti –Shanti -Shanti*' in our high pitched voices. The noise of the forks and spoons would, take over and sounded like the sudden 'roll of drums,' as the boys all addressed the food served on our metal thalis.

On a memorable evening for me, Mr. Apte the Music Master held an impromptu Inter house singing competition. Two boys from each House, were to sing a short song from amongst the semi-classical bhajans we were practicing every day at the morning and evening assemblies. Midway in the evening, I suddenly found myself pushed into the circle of light around Mr. Apte, who was providing the background notes on the *tamboora*. Out of sheer nervousness, I shut my eyes tightly and let the sound of the *tamboora* take over as I sang a few lines describing the coming of monsoons rain-bearing clouds. I now only recollect the words –"*kare kare badal umarawat* —"(dark rain clouds fill the sky). I was quite thrilled to be told later that evening that my singing had been judged the best that evening.

By and by we got promoted to the higher classes. In the senior classes, we were only a bare few and as such found ourselves appointed prefects and other school duties. Somehow I got nominated as the School Head boy during 1951.

Gen Cariappa's visit (1950)

Red Carpet Welcome

During this period we had the then Commander-in-Chief of the Army, General K M Cariappa visit the school informally. He had driven up in an open jeep to the southern end of the lake at *Talital* from the plains, where our senior School Master, Shri Mohan Chand Tiwari, accompanied by two of us senior boys, had met the General and had invited him to visit the school. In his smart uniform, the General glanced uphill at the barely visible location of the hilltop school, and accepted the invitation.

On the appointed day the General rode up on a pony, with the local groom hanging onto the tail of the animal. This unseemly practice, enabled the groom to keep up with the horse on steep gradients and was the general practice at Nainital. No cars were allowed beyond the southern end of the lake or uphill roads. Only the Governor's car, a sedate black Humber Hawk sedan, was permitted on the road leading to the Government House on the opposite side of the lake. There was an excellent network of bridle paths in Nainital even then, and our school was connected to the eastern upper one, but had a steep ascent in the final approach.

Classmate Maneege Sateesh Rao and I received the General a little down slope, and escorted him to where the Principal and other members of the staff were waiting. As we guided the pony along, leading it by the bridle, the General asked Sateesh and me

as to what we wanted to do after finishing school. Sateesh said that he aspired to become a doctor of medicine. Some years later he settled in Cambridge as the resident doctor there. On my part I told the visitor that I aspired to Join the Army.

Wearing a smart blue blazer, the General addressed the staff and us students in his clipped 'roman' Hindustani. He sounded like an Englishman, and addressed us *"ustadoan aur bachoan ----"* without a trace of self consciousness or hesitation. He was India's first Commander-in-Chief and carried himself with great aplomb and dignity. His aide was a smart Sikh officer, wearing the maroon pugri of the Parachute Regiment. Attentive and poised, the Chief and his aide made a good impression on us school boys.

General Cariappa was the Colonel of The Rajput Regiment, into which I was later commissioned in June 1956. He had retired as the Chief by the time I joined the Regiment, but remained it's Honorary Colonel thereafter until he passed away in 1993. In 1992, a year before he died, I paid him a farewell visit after retiring as the Sixth Colonel (1987-91) of his Regiment. This being an elected appointment of a "Father Figure" of the Regiment enjoyed a great deal of prestige and honour. I was the first post War officer from within the Regiment to be elected thus to this appointment in 1986-87. The Regiment had almost thirty battalions by the time I got the task of handling this vital and honorific task.

In late retirement, Cariappa was made a Field Marshal in 1986 which gave The Rajputs an aura of its own, having him as an Honorary Colonel (a life long Honour).

In February 1992, a few months after my own retirement and on relinquishing the appointment of Colonel of his Regiment, I paid the ailing and ageing Field Marshal at the Air Force Hospital at Bangalore, my humble personal regard, and respect for the Father figure he had been for Army in general and for my Regiment in particular.

I told him how we had relaid the War memorial and main parade ground at the Regimental Centre at Fatehgarh, and named it "Cariappa Complex" in the Field Marshal's honour. I told him of how as a school boy I had been so struck by his personality and had always taken him as a role model as a soldier.

I also told him how I had commanded a Rajput battalion in the 1971 War for the Liberation of Bangladesh, which had earned the 'Battle Honour of Akhaura'. I felt no hesitation in telling him that under my stewardship the Regiment was looking up in every manner.

JOINING THE ARMY

DEHRADUN – THE NATIONAL DEFENCE ACADEMY

The Indian Military Academy (IMA) in Premnagar; had been in existence since 1932, and was located next to the vast campus of the Forest Research Institute in the western part of the Doon Valley. The IMA was the 'Sandhurst' of the Indian Army, and was beautifully laid out around the imposing Chetwode Building and adjoining the Drill Square. Field Marshal Sir Philip Chetwode was the Commander- in- Chief in India after whom the main Building was named and had in his inauguration address on 10 December 1932 given out the meaningful credo for the officers of the Indian Army being commissioned from the Academy which began in the following words --

" *The Safety, Honour and Welfare of your Country come first, always and every time".*

In July 1952 when I joined, the existing campus of the IMA provided the 'Military Wing' of the National Defence Academy (NDA) which had its 'Joint Services Wing' (JSW) set up in Clement Town, a few miles away, astride the Suswa nala. The Suswa becomes a river as it drains out of the valley, cutting through the low Sal jungle covered Shivaliks hills to the south. The co-location of the two 'Wings' at Dehradun was an interim measure as the elaborate NDA campus was under construction at Khadakvasla near Pune. For the initial batches, two years at the JSW were to be followed up with two further years at the respective Service Academies. Army cadets at that time passed out of Joint Services Wing to join the Military Wing, thus remaining in Dehradun before commissioning as officers.

Later, when NDA moved to Khadakvasla in July 1954, the 'Military Wing' remained at Dehradun and in due course resumed its original name of 'Indian Military Academy'. All this got changed later to three years at the NDA at Pune and a year at the IMA for the Army Cadets at Dehradun.

Having been selected at the Selection Centre located at Bangalore, I reported for the JSW for its 8th Course at its Clement Town location in southern Doon Valley in July 1952. The Wing was housed in accommodations which had been used earlier as a large Italian Prisoner of War Camp during World War II, and was of drab temporary hutment-type construction. Our rooms were called 'cabins' in deferment to the Navy. We were organised into 'squadrons' and subdivided into 'divisions'.

Central and dominating the whole cadet squadron hutments, was a large drill square which had an imposing Naval Quarter-deck installed on a platform which served as a saluting base for the visiting VIP. The tall Quarter deck served as a giant flag mast, with the national flag flown at the very top. The three Services and the NDA flags were displayed from a lower yard arm. World War II relics, a 'Spitfire' fighter aircraft and a 'Honey' Stuart light Tank were war time trophies placed at the entrance of the Drill Square.

Our classes for academic subjects were in a separate area, and an elaborate riding school and physical training grounds besides play fields and a swimming pool were provided.

The two years of the JSW were a period of bonding and smartening up to instil a military bearing in us. It involved a constant effort and struggle to keep up with the spit and polish that the Academy demanded and was ruthlessly enforced by the drill staff, both on and off the parade ground. We wore well-starched, smart khaki drill uniforms for foot drill, which was conducted under the supervision of a British Regimental Sergeant and a host of drill instructors. During the evenings we changed from games kit into our mess kit. In summer it consisted of a white 'monkey' jacket with a red cummerbund for the evening meals. In winter we wore Blue Patrols. The Blue Patrols were tailor made ceremonial dress made of blue serge material. Shinning brass buttons and the red piping on the trousers were distinctive.

A change wrought in us by the precision and perfection demanded of us on the drill square, the habit of instant obedience, the bone-shaking stamping of feet in unison. We were soon quite transformed from heterogeneous schoolboys to smart look alike cadets.

Our syllabus for academics was roughly of intermediate college standard. A civilian instructional staff under a principal looked after our educational training. Hardly any military subjects were included. Some few Army Education Corps officers were also posted on the teaching faculty for some classes.

I had always had difficulty in mathematics. It did not help that I was clubbed in class '8-F' under a Army Education Corps Instructor, Major French. Cadets were clubbed as per aptitudes starting from '8-A' to '8-F'. Being in the lowest group was a serious handicap. Obviously, Major French, too, was a "mathematician" like us and spent more time ensuring the ventilation of the room rather then addressing our collective lack of aptitude for the subject. At the end of the two years I managed to just scrape through. It perhaps helped that I was given the Cadet appointment of a "Sergeant- Major" by Major Kunwar Chand Singh, my Squadron

Commander. I suspect the following incident helped in bringing this about.

One afternoon, we took our road walk and run into the shady Sal jungle which was adjacent to the JSW campus. We had moved along a forest road into the depth of the Suswa block. At one spot, on a bend in the forest road, I lingered on the roadside on recognising the pug marks of a tigress. She must have passed that way the previous night. As I bent over looking at the pugmark, I realised that my Squadron Commander, Major Kunwar Chand Singh had come up silently behind me and was looking over my shoulder. Major Kunwar Chand was a Rajput from Rajasthan with a bushy mustache and thick eyebrows and was a man of few words. Soft-spoken and a shikari, he asked me about the pugmarks I was looking at. I must have impressed him with my knowledge on the subject acquired in the earlier years from my father in the central Indian jungles. I suspect he helped me out later by giving me the rotational appointment of Squadron Sergeant Major which at the time of passing out gave me some amount of protection. It meant that I escaped relegation (relegation meant loss of six months).

Shikar was a much sought after club activity in the JSW. I had managed to get selected for a trip out for a jungle fowl shoot on a weekend. The shooting block reserved for us was on the west of the Mohan Pass (in Sahranpur District). The major excitement of the day was that a well-fed leopard broke out of a beat. Luckily nothing untoward happened. Major Chand Singh had been on this outing as the officer in charge. I had been at the other end of the beat and never saw the leopard. There was considerable excitement over the sighting of the animal.

However, it was during this first outing that I met a young local guide and shikari, Nathu. He was employed by the Academy Shikar Club. He seemed to be only a little older than me at that time and I got to know him a lot better later, when he switched over to the Shikar Club activities of the Military Wing as the

local Shikari and guide. We were later to share many adventures and close calls in the later years. He lived close to the Asarori or Karwapani Shooting Block embracing the southern Shivalik hill slopes of the Doon Valley. He remained a boyish, clear eyed and cheerful friend all through the years.

Before moving on to the Military Wing stage, I would like to narrate what could be called the 'Blue Streak' incident of our two-years stay at The Joint Services Wing at Clement Town. A coursemate cadet was confounded with an unexpected and sudden problem of not having an underwear to be worn under his khaki drill shorts. Time was short and running out. The cadet resorted to quickly improvising by pulling up both legs of the full length of his blue striped cotton pyjamas and liberally using several safety pins he had handy to hold things in place, tucked up under the khaki shorts. The cadet seemed set for the days drill parade.

All went well for some time until Regimental Sergeant Major (RSM) Ayling of the renowned British Grenadier Guards, yelled his head off on seeing one leg of the cadet's pyjamas getting undone. The safety pins had not reckoned with the jarring foot drill and the violent repeated stamping of the feet. One leg of the blue striped pyjama slid down, leading to the tirade by the tall Grenadier Guardsman RSM.

The cadet was next seen doubling around the Parade ground with the 'Blue Streak' leg of his pyjama being joined by the other. It had proved too much for the 'safety pins' to hold up the stuffed pyjamas. Both legs of the striped blue pyjamas were now visible to all of us on the drill square that day. The cadet had a hard time living down the 'Blue Streak' event. The red tip of his nose looked redder than before as he doubled passed us, trying to overcome his embarrassment.

Regimental Sergeant Major Ayling of the British Grenadier Guards wore his red-banded peak hat with aplomb and his voice quite thundered in our ears as he made us respond to his words

Final Steps — JSW passing out
(Left to Right): K.B. Deswal, Lamba, Bajpai, Author, Ajai Singh and Mukund Natu.

of command. It would be a breathless moment when marching off from parade as we would respond in unison, coming to an earth-shaking crashing halt when ordered to do so. Sometimes it would not work, and some fumbling would lead to a disjointed shuffle. Ayling's voice would thunder "I have the loudest voice in Dehradun" with a tone of reproach. He once stopped short at "I have the loudest voice," - - which one of the cadets from somewhere completed after a brief pause –"in Dehradun, Sergeant Major!" Ayling was not amused.

THE MILITARY WING

After passing out from the Joint Services Wing in June 1954, we reported to the Military Wing for further training. Following our passing out, the 'JSW' at Clement Town at Dehradun was wound up and shifted to Khadakvasla near Pune to form the National Defence Academy (NDA). Meanwhile, our batch spent two years at the Military Wing at Dehradun (which later reverted to being called The Indian Military Academy- IMA). We graduated from there in June 1956 and were commissioned as second lieutenants (2/Lt) into various arms and services.

At the Military Wing I was lucky to be assigned to Meiktila Company, which had Major Gurbaksh Gill, a 'Gunner' officer, as its Company Commander. Major Gill, apart from being an outstanding sportsman, was a very keen shikari. He took note of my enthusiasm for the sport and having had some exposure to big game shikar at home. Nathu, our guide and local shikari, whom we had met in the JSW at Clement Town earlier, and I managed almost always to be included in the Shikar Club ventures.

I found that after a hesitant start, I soon got quite adept at wielding a shotgun in the *'murghi'* (red jungle fowl) shoots that were organised during the shooting season, which extended over the later half of the month during the shooting season. The Military Wing Shikar Club was usually allotted the nearby 'Karwapani – Asarori' shooting block. Licences and permits were strictly respected and inspected by the forest department staff.

THE MILITARY WING

Chetwode Hall, Indian Military Academy

Since we were usually allotted the same shooting block, we got to know the lie of the ground fairly well.

'*Murghi*' or red jungle fowl shikar was new for me. At home I had mainly been exposed to big game shikar with my father, and organised bird shooting needed a quick eye and accurate shooting to tackle the fast flying bird across the line of guns as they flashed past, barely giving you a fleeting opportunity. A certain amount of anticipation and quick responses were essential.

The sal forest and its fringes of the Karwapani block were systematically 'beaten' for *murghi*, using a handful of local beaters organised by Nathu, the guide cum shikari. There was a fair amount of wild '*ber*' bushes, the thorny patches of which next to the sal forest, yielded a fair number of red jungle fowl, mixed sometimes with some *kaleej* pheasants. Three to four guns would take up a line, along a forest road or fire lane, spaced about 40 to 50 yards apart. Care has to be exercised that flanking guns were kept in sight to avoid shooting accidents. Usually a patch of jungle was not beaten more than once every two months or so.

The Karwapani-Asarori Shooting Block was concurrently also booked for big game for the Shikar Club during the shooting season. Though used mainly for *murghi* beats, as described, Nathu Shikari would routinely tie up a buffalo calf bait for a tiger at a couple of select spots within the block. Major Gill kept this more select sport under a strict wrap. Nathu would bring in the news of a 'kill' if it occurred by midday.

In my second term I got appointed as the Gentlemen Cadet Secretary of the Shikar Club. Major Gill began reposing a lot of confidence in me and on more then one occasion had sent me in the afternoons to check on Nathu's work on horse-back from the Academy Stables. I quite enjoyed the ride along with an accompanying riding instructor.

Once it had so transpired, that Major Gill had once asked me on one such trip, to check out a particular machan that had been set up at one of the tie-up spots in anticipation, to save on time in the event of the kill taking place.

Inspite of my limited experience, I had concurred with Major Gill's observation, that the particular machan in question seemed uncomfortably close to where the bait was tied. On an earlier occasion, when Major Gill had used the same machan over a kill, the tiger had failed to turn up as it seemed to have got suspicious. It was this same machan which we had expressed unease about that was involved in a serious shikar incident that occurred a little later.

We were in our final term in the spring of 1956, when it happened. It involved Major Gurbaksh Gill and Lt Col Harkesh Gehlot of the Grenadiers. Nathu the shikari cum guide was with them at the time, when both these officers got severely mauled by a young male tiger they had wounded in the previous night's sit up. It was the same machan at the track junction in some thick sal jungle that I have alluded to earlier

THE MILITARY WING

Lakhimpur Khevi – 1955 – GC Bahuguna, Major Gurbux Gill – Nathu (Shikari)

Since I was familiar with the ground and the general setting of the event, I will attempt to briefly reconstruct the event from the telltale signs that I got to see when I accompanied Nathu back to the site of the incident to help bring back the dead tiger after the event. My reconstruction of the event is also based on having several times later talked to both the officers about the event whilst they were recovering from their wounds in the Military Hospital at Dehradun. They were in the Hospital for almost a month after the event. Nathu Shikari had also told me of what had happened as he had been an active participant.

As the individual's perception of the critical events differs, one has to give allowance to some distortion in the telling of the tale.

THE ASARORI TIGER

Almost a year before the event of the severe mauling of Major Gill and Colonel Gehlot, it so happened that we had a close enough brush with probably the same tiger. We were a two Gentlemen Cadets (GCs) team, sitting together in separate ground hide, waiting for wild boars to cross over from the main jungle through a wide fire-break lane. The Karwapani-Timli forest road ran along the edge of the scrub jungle the boars had to enter before they could get to the cultivation beyond. A second team of GC Surajit Choudhry with another Gentlemen Cadet, and my similar team had occupied widely separated ground hides along the edge of the forest road in the shadowy fringe of the scrub jungle with the hope of detecting and intercepting the boars as they tried crossing the wide open fire lane.

As it got dark and the time for the boar crossings went by, my twosome got up from our concealed position to walk back to the other hide beyond which our vehicle was waiting for us. As I started off with a torch in my hand, I saw a long grey shape hurry diagonally across from the shadowy fringe on our side into the main jungle from about forty yards or so from us. It certainly was not a boar or any other smaller animal. My companion and I froze and stood still, holding our breath for several minutes. The presence of a tiger does things to one's breathing and heartbeat. It was ambling along in the shady fringe on our side of the road, until it saw us emerge from the hide in the dim moonlight. He would have passed very close to us if we had not luckily moved out. Surajit had already got to the vehicle, having either seen or sensed the presence of the tiger on the prowl.

The Asarori Tiger was a 3 or 4 year old male who would some times visit the Asarori- Karwapani shooting block from across the Shivalik Hills. The tie up of a buffalo calf as a bait at a suitable site was done with the hope of this wandering tiger taking the bait tied up by Nathu Shikari at a selected track junction located in some fairly thick sal surroundings. A machan had already been constructed at the site to avoid disturbing the tiger who was expected to lie up close to the kill. On an earlier occasion the same tiger had got suspicious of the noises made in setting up the machan and had remained in the vicinity but did not show up on the kill. That would explain the pre-prepared machan at the site.

Major Gill was an experienced big game shikari. He owned a .450/400 double-barrelled rifle, firing a cordite driven 300-grain bullet. A suitable weapon for taking on big game like tiger. The Shikar Club of the Academy also had a similar. 450/400 double barrelled rifle, which on this occasion was being used by Colonel Gehlot. Major Gill's experience wise was the "senior" shikari of the two. Colonel Gehlot was new at the game, but very keen to 'bag' a tiger. Major Gill, a Gunner officer, was a trifle impatient by nature, an outstanding athlete and sportsman. Gehlot was a laid back Infantryman of the Grenadiers Regiment. He spoke with a slight lisp which we Gentlemen Cadets found most impressive. I remember him once briefing us during an outdoor exercise with a wet cigarette in his mouth as if he didn't seem to notice the heavy downpour of rain. He seemed like a character out of the book 'From Here to Eternity'.

Gehlot had prevailed on Gill to take him along when Nathu Shikari reported the news of the kill. They got to the site well in time and settled down quietly on the pre-prepared machan. It was perhaps understood that Gehlot would take the first shot, once the tiger settled down to feeding on the kill. Both the officers had suitable torches clamped on to their respective .450/400

DBBL rifles. Nathu Shikari left the two officers after they were comfortably settled and went back to await developments to where their vehicle, a 15 cwt truck, was waiting.

The tiger arrived on the kill after darkness had set in. Owing to the closeness of the machan, the heavy breathing was clearly audible to both the officers in the dark. As the tiger started to feed, Gehlot, it appears, took the first shot, which was followed by Gill's hurried supporting effort. Something seems to have gone wrong as the tiger with a loud roar, had disappeared from the patch of torch light.

The wounded tiger had leapt away into the surrounding darkness. Both the officers took time to absorb the situation. It is more than likely and probable that the two shikari officers, who had to stay on the machan for the remainder of the night, talked between themselves, discussing what had happened in whispers. The wounded tiger had remained in the neighbourhood, occasionally venting his anger by growling and groaning. The wounded animal seemed to be moving from place to place in the vicinity, during the night.

Major Gill, the more experienced of the two, may have felt that Gehlot's shot had been taken in some haste. Nothing could be done about it, however, but the dangerous task of following up the wounded tiger in the thick sal jungle in the morning was a daunting task ahead. The grim situation they were faced with could not be taken lightly.

Next morning when Nathu Shikari arrived at the machan, a plan of action was hastily drawn up. Both the officers had carefully reloaded their double-barreled .450-400 rifles, ready for instant use. Besides, Nathu Shikari was armed with a double barreled shotgun, loaded with buckshot. Nathu had the crucial job of looking for the blood trail in the followup. The tension can be imagined as the party of three set out. Both the officers were still in uniform as they had come directly from work the previous day. Perhaps the requirement of getting back to the Academy for the day's work also led to some haste in handling the dangerous task of following up the wounded tiger. It was a case of asking for trouble and they headed for it in a big way.

The party of three followed the blood trail, led by Nathu. They had heard the tiger moving about and growling intermittently from varying distances during the night. They had been at it in a pretty keyed up state for the nerve-racking task in the oppressive heat of the thick Sal jungle. There was no scope for haste or impatience.

They turned back, retracing their steps to get back to the area in the vicinity of the machan. Nathu was now trailing behind, when the tiger unexpectedly suddenly burst upon Major Gill with a loud roar. As the tiger leapt at Gill, both the officers discharged their respective rifles at almost point blank range- firing the four barrels in the melee. In the tense situation, the recoil of a heavy rifle, this possibility of "jerking off" both barrels, is a nightmarish situation. Nathu too discharged his buckshots in some haste, which mercifully seems to have missed the enraged tiger and the two officers grappling with the beast. It could have caused a serious accident in the tight situation. Meanwhile, one of the rifle bullets in the melee at almost point-blank range, had luckily struck the tiger in the face, breaking his jaw at the joint.

The tiger went initially for Gill, leaping at him and slashing at Gills head with his left foreleg, knocking his pugree aside and tearing his left ear away with his claws. Major Gill fell backwards while the tiger began chewing at one of his arms. He was still holding on to his rifle, for which he was carrying spare bullets in his Smock-Denizen parachute jacket. While falling backwards he had slipped partially under the tiger bringing up his knee against the stomach of the animal. The tiger now quickly switched his attention to Gills legs.

Meanwhile Gehlot stepped forward and jabbing the tigers flank with his rifle and attempted to fire his second barrel. You can imagine the horror of the situation when Gehlot realised

that he had fired off both barrels at the charging tiger. Maybe the suddenness of the situation and the recoil of the weapon had contributed. The tiger now left Gill to attack Gehlot, whom he knocked down and began to bite at the top of his head. One of his canine teeth sank deep into the back of the Colonel's skull, through the beret he was wearing.

Gill, realising that he too had fired off both his weapon's barrels in the sudden encounter, managed to pull out a spare cartridge from his jacket and quickly reload the rifle. He faced some difficulty pushing forward the safety catch of the weapon owing to the blood flowing making things slippery. The point- blank heart shot knocked the tiger dead. The shattered jaw had caused deep and severe injuries to both the officers. What would have happened if the tigers jaw had been unhurt is difficult to imagine.

Both the officers and Nathu managed to get to the waiting vehicle before the shock set in and drove straight to the Military Hospital in Dehradun Cantonment. Both survived to later rise to the rank of major general in their respective arm of service in later years.

In writing about this event after more then fifty five years have elapsed, I may have made some inadvertent mistake in narrating the details. Essentially the saga of courage in such adversity displayed by the two stands out. Fortune did favour the brave as the smashed jaw of the tiger allowed them to survive. It also stood out that double barrel heavy rifles are better replaced by shotguns for such close quarter encounters. A magazine rifle may be a preferred option. But things can go very wrong in such situations.

The Asarori or Karwapani Tiger was later mounted as a trophy with the head mounted by Van Ingen & Van Ingen's of Mysore, the best taxidermist in the country. The Trophy was displayed for several decades thereafter in the Cadets Cafe in the Indian Military Academy. Several generation of young officers commissioned into the Army would remember the trophy and the saga of courage associated with it.

COMMISSIONING

Just a few days before the Asarori or Karwapani episode, I had accompanied Major Gill on an impromptu afternoon's murghi shoot on the express desire of the venerable Deputy Commandant, Colonel Ranbir Singh. The Colonel was awarded a Military Cross (MC) for having rescued a wounded British colleague in the grim fighting against the Japanese at Kohima in the Second World War. It was said of him "Colonel Ranbir could hardly merge with the crowd. Authority sat on him naturally and he looked a leader, every inch of him, twirling his moustache and officers' cane with some natural dignity and importance." We hardly got to know him as Gentlemen Cadets, but something about his aloof personality was such that we GCs held him in awe. He owned a war disposal jeep, which his Rajput Regiment driver, Naik Bhagwan Singh, sporting the Colonel's regiment's royal blue and maroon hackle on his beret , drove with conspicuous panache.

We took the Chakrata road, turning off North towards the jungle-clad lower slopes of *Mussourie* hills, taking one of the dirt roads running along the edge of one of the stony, dry watercourse which sheltered some jungly *murghis* (red jungle fowl) in the bushes. These birds would feed in the scattered fields through which the dirt road ran in the morning and evening hours.

That afternoon we were just three 'guns' for the improvised effort and we spaced ourselves about 40 yards apart, along the road. The handful of beaters beat the bushes besides the nala's edges, hurtling stones and beating the foliage with bamboo sticks. The hidden jungle fowl would flush out with an sudden burst as they tried to fly across the dirt road to seek safety in the abundant bushes scattered beyond. The 'guns' had to try to shoot down the fast flying bird as it flashed past high over the road. It required some skill and luck to bring down a *murghi* in full flight.

Inspite of waiting expectantly with a thumb on the safety catch, the shikari was apt to be surprised with the sudden flushing of the bird. Often the shots failed to bring down the fast-flying target which can only be hit if the correct lead is given, which has to take into account of the angle of the flight of the game-bird. Even a fifty-percent success, is considered creditable.

We flushed only a few birds that afternoon. One of these flashed past Colonel Ranbir, the Deputy Commandant, who managed to take his right hand off from tending his moustaches and brought off a good shot to knock down the bird which fell down in the foliage. From where I was on a flank, I clearly saw the bird being knocked over and plummeting down into the leafy foliage.

The beaters failed to locate the fallen bird. The Colonel seemed baffled at not finding the bird, and turned to move away muttering something about the bird probably being a 'runner'. I noticed the disappointment writ on his proud soldier's face.

I got to where he had been standing in the beat, as the spent cartridge ejected by him marked the spot. I then mentally visualized the flight trajectory of the bird he had knocked over. Sure enough after looking carefully, I caught sight of the dead bird dangling by its neck in the fork of a branch. No wonder the beaters had failed to notice this, as they searched for the fallen bird on the ground. The coloring of the *murghi* also blended completely with the foliage.

The Colonel's face lit up at my bringing the bird out for him. He then asked me the all important question as to which arm of the Army and which Regiment I was aspiring to go to. Somehow,

the Colonel seemed to have been so impressed by the incident narrated, that he selected me to go to his own Battalion.

Later, when driving back that afternoon, I looked more closely at driver Naik Bhagwan Singh's Royal Blue and Maroon feathered hackle and the symmetrically crafted badge of The Rajput Regiment that he wore so proudly on his beret. He still wore the old British days, 'Lion on the Crown' and 'VII' Numbering in the cap badge.

On 3rd June 1956, I was commissioned as a second lieutenant into Colonel Ranbir Singh's own Second Battalion of The Rajputs. After a month's leave at Bombay with my parents, I was to report to The Rajput Regimental Centre located at Fatehgarh in the heart of Uttar Pradesh for a fortnight's introductory stay.

FATEHGARH – THE REGIMENTAL CENTRE

The fortnight at Fatehgarh was a complete anti-climatic introduction to what I had expected. The Regimental Centre was a sleepy and dusty, dull set up. It was difficult enough a place to get to owing to the lack of rail connection, but every thing about the place seemed seedy and listless. Located on the banks of the Ganga River, it seemed to be as backward as could be. It came as a great shock to start one's regimental life in such a lack lustre manner. Nobody seemed to care to even introduce me to the few officers posted there. All in all, it was a very poor introduction to what was to be such an important part of the life I had to lead in the Regiment.

Largely left to myself, I spent as much of my time in trying to imbibe as much of the history and background of the old trophies and silver in the Officers Mess. 'Lake and Victory' seemed an odd and unexplained part of what was prominently displayed on the banners and even the glassware in the Mess. No one seemed to know or care for all the valuable shikar and other trophies.

It remained a mystery as to why I was the lone officer commissioned in June 1956 to get this fortnight's exposure at the Centre. All my batchmates had reported directly to their battalions at the initial joining. Perhaps it helped in the long run as I formed a lasting impression of Fatehgarh, and realized that it needed to be made the proud 'Home' of the Regiment in later years.

Later, as I got interested in the history of the Rajput Regiment, I realized that the 'Regiment' as such was formed out of several original, individual Bengal Infantry battalions raised by the British since 1778. Six of the original units that had survived the events of 1857, had been clubbed together to form the Regiment when it was set up as such with the Centre being located at Fatehgarh in UP. In fact, one of the six had been made the Centre in 1921. All these units of the Regiment, now wore a common regimental badge. Royal blue, old gold and maroon were the designated colors of the Regimental flag.

Each of the original battalions celebrated events of the past in which they had distinguished themselves. For instance, 'Lake and Victory' was emblazoned on a special and the unique distinction earned by a battalion under General Gerald Lake in the Battle of Patparganj on 6 September 1803. This was a desperate battle against the Marathas, fought in the area of present day NOIDA Golf Course. Five units of Lake's force were awarded a special distinction of carrying an extra Honorary Colour. Of these five, only 1 Rajput had survived.

My fortnight's introductory sojourn at Fatehgarh set me into a mindset of wanting to learn as much of the past history of the Regiment which I had become a part of. During the Second World War the Regiment had been expanded with many new units. Many had been retained even after postwar demobilization. Further, some of the State Forces battalions also became a part of the Regiment. In later years, as the need arose, new raising were carried out from time to time.

JOINING THE BATTALION

The Second Battalion of the Rajput Regiment was located in a camp near the Basantar River, in Samba when I joined them in July 1956. We were living in tentage in the low hills west of the river. The Shivalik hills were dry and covered with thorny *Babool* or *Kikar* jungle. Cut up by ravines, the area was difficult to negotiate as I soon, learnt the hard way during the introductory exercises I was put through. July and August were very uncomfortable and muggy wet months. However, I managed to get along well with the *Gujar* boys of my platoon in the toughening up process. The *Gujars* of the Battalion had come from the 8th Punjab *Regiment* (allotted to Pakistan) at the time of Partition.

Havildar Kamal Ram had been awarded a Victoria Cross with 4/8 Punjab in the Sangro River fighting in Italy. Subedar Desh Raj, a Gujar Platoon commander, had been awarded a Military Cross in the same battle. I learnt to recognize the campaign ribbons worn by the veterans as it allowed me to differentiate between those who had served in Italy or in Burma.

General K M Cariappa, had been the first Colonel of the Rajput Regiment, and as the First Commander-in-Chief had introduced a Bengali Company in place of one of the *Gujars* during the readjustment following the split as a result of partition. By 1956, when I joined the 2nd Battalion the new intake of Bengalis had somewhat settled down in the unit. These were the first Bengalis in the infantry.

JOINING THE BATTALION

The Second Battalion was then commanded by Lt Col Harkesh Singh Bolina. He had come to the Regiment from the Kumoani's where he had been decorated with a Vir Chakra, deservedly earned in the battle on the Pandu Feature in the Uri Sector (with 4 Kumoan in the J&K operations as a Major). I was placed as a 'Company Officer' and assigned as a platoon commander in the *Gujar* Company (Bravo). An elaborate programme put me through a toughening routine, which at the height of summer and the monsoons was unpleasant and hard going. During this period I must have done well enough with the men and seemed to have established a bonding with the rank and file which is so essential in Infantry soldiering.

Barely a month had elapsed when I got into trouble. On a weekend, having a rare moment of idling in my tent, I had drawn a rough cartoon, depicting the 'Zoo' of officers as their appointments. The code signs used were well known, 'Tiger', denoted the Commanding Officer (CO), 'Lamb', for the second-in- Command, 'Lion', for Adjutant and so on. All appointments were accordingly referred to in radio speech or when referring to them on the telephone. I had in a flippant moment drawn a cartoon depicting these appointments in the battalion. Major Qamar Hasnain, one of the senior majors of the Battalion, chanced to see this rough drawing in my tent. Without considering the consequence of his action, Major Hasnain took the sketch and pinned it on the Officers' Mess notice board.

2/Lts were considered as mutes, to be sometimes 'seen' on the fringes, but never to be 'heard'. I had somehow broken this unwritten convention. Lt Col H S Bolina did not like my sketch of him as the 'Tiger' in the centre of the drawing. His pugree used to progressively get untidier as he would push it up to hear the telephone better. Somehow my sketch captured this and caused serious offence. As luck would have it, the Brigade Headquarters (located nearby) thrust an unexpected and unwanted vacancy

for a 'Young Officers' Weapons course due to commence in mid-September. For an infantry officer this is the first 'career' course and considered vital as it is meant to make the officer proficient in the handling of all platoon weapons and in the imparting of such training to the rank and file.

The 'rifle',pistol and 'light machine gun' firing to achieve minimum standards was essential to qualify on the Platoon Weapons Course. It was usual practice to prepare a young officer by making him fire these weapons under supervision and guidance at the rifle ranges in the unit. An 'Instructors' grade if achieved by an infantry officer was highly sought after. Captains Pant and Raghbir Sain of the Battalion had both got this qualification in their past and were much admired for that. Besides proficiency in the handling and firing these platoon weapons, we were required to learn to conduct classes for the men. 'IPs' or instructional practices were laid down and 'precis' printed which had to be learnt by rote. I was quite handicapped in this as I was rushed into going on the course . Consequently, I could never do very well on the course.

Before leaving from Samba for the course, Lieut Tarun Ghosh, the senior subaltern and an excellent football player, and 2/Lt Raghunath Jaswal my immediate senior by six months (from the ranks and a good sportsman) seemed very upset with this development, as they felt it could have a negative impact on my career. The CO (Commanding Officer) was in fact punishing me for the cheeky sketch.

The senior subaltern, Tarun and I would every evening tramp back over the Basanter River Bridge, after the days 'training events', which was carried out on the Mawa dirt track leading towards the border. I had a pocket mouth organ and could play the Grenadier Guards march-past tune on it to the cadence of our boots on the wooden planks on the bridges' foot path. Almost every evening we would be about midway across the bridge when the sound of the evening 'Retreat' would come floating across from the Battalion's

location on the far side of the river. Sepoy Shree Ram, the bugler, otherwise a mousy little and unimpressive looking soldier, could do something with that bugle call that was beyond description. Both Tarun and I would feel a little sad at the passing of the day. I would get a lump in the throat by the way bugler Shree Ram sounded the bugle call in the gathering gloom of dusk.

As for the sudden weapons course at Mhow being thrust on me, I was mistakenly quite happy with the development, as I was getting a little bored and worn out with the repetitive nature of the daily slog. Being a reasonable rifle shot as a shikari, it made me confident of managing on the Course. Company Havildar Major Kishan Singh gave me a few days hurried exposure to firing practices on the rifle ranges. I found the range practices quite different from the use of sport weapons.

*****

Pathankot was the starting station in those days. Travelling by train in uniform, with a rifle slung on my shoulder and a .38 Calibre (S & W) revolver in a holster, I arrived home in Bombay for a couple of days unexpected break before reporting at the Infantry School located at Mhow, near Indore in Central India. My parents were most surprised by my coming home so soon.

Bombay (Mumbai) to Ratlam was an overnight trip by the main line broad-gauge train. A Parsee lady co-passenger had also boarded the train at Mumbai for Ratlam. I had noticed a look of amusement on her face, seeing me strut along with my weapons. Realising that we were further travelling together, I helped her get her baggage into the compartment onto the metre-gauge train that was to take us to Mhow, where the Infantry School was located. I realized that she was joining her husband who was posted at the Infantry School.

When we reached Mhow, I got busy collecting my baggage and as I alighted from the train, the Parsee lady introduced me to 'Sam', her husband who had come to receive her. He was in

some kind of a uniform with a red band on his jungle hat. Since he wore no badges of rank, I was unsure for a minute or so. From his striking youthful looks, with a prominent beak like nose and moustache, I could just guess that he was a very senior officer. As a very raw young 2 /Lt, I did not know what I should do or say.

The lady was Siloo, the wife of the Commandant, Brigadier 'Sam' SHFJ Maneckshaw. He had come to receive her at the station. She thereafter most graciously invited me to call on them at their Flag Staff Residence once I was settled. I was quite taken in by all this and could not quite grasp or understand the sudden lucky exposure.

The following day, Brigadier (Sam) Maneckshaw, as the Commandant of the Infantry School, made the usual welcoming remarks customarily made on such occasions for the fresh Weapons Course officers assembled for the purpose. I recognized him after having seen him at the railway station the previous day.

At the end of his few minutes address, he paused and asked the audience if there were any questions. Promptly, a portly sikh officer, Captain Surat Singh of the Sikh Regiment got up and said that in the earlier briefing by the administrative staff, he had been told that all student officers were to be charged Rs 2 for the duration of our stay, for being given a bucket of warm water in the morning before the day's activities. Captain Surat said that he was accustomed to bathing with cold water, and did not need the hot water being charged for. The Commandant with barely a pause brought the house down by suggesting to the Captain sahib –" that he was free to collect his warm water and let it cool off before he had his bath." The Brigadier's spontaneous response was said in such a manner that it invoked instant good humoured laughter from us all. There was not a trace of malice in the sharp witted remark of the Commandant. 'Sam' was to become a much respected icon figure of the Indian Army in the 1971 War for the Bangladesh Liberation War.

In due course I got invited to the Flag Staff House by Mrs Maneckshaw, who recognized me amongst the young lot hanging around at the Central India Club, during a weekend dance. I was amongst several other young officers invited for lunch at the Commandant's residence on a weekend. The personal warmth and bonhomie was a striking feature of the afternoon. The two lovely daughters, Sherry and Maya, with Siloo Maneckshaw quite bowled us over with their charm and hospitality. Sam Maneckshaw mingled with us effortlessly. He sat down beside us on the wooden floor and told us of his earlier days in the Frontier Force Rifles unit he had been assigned to in his earlier service. He even showed us some yellowing photographs of himself wearing extra long khaki shorts and oversized solar pith hats in vogue in those days.

Even then, inspite of my fresh induction into the Army in general, I was most taken in by the easy wit and sparkle of Sam Manekshaw. He seemed to enjoy soldiering and was completely at ease with us. He seemed to be a natural leader, with no rank consciousness. I could sense that he was great role model for the Army and felt lucky and privileged to have had a close look at him and his family so early in my career.

I managed to do well enough on the Course. I was easily the junior most officer attending the Infantry Weapons Course, and managed to make many friends from the other lot attending various Courses, both at the Infantry and Signal Schools, co-located at Mhow. I found that officers from the armoured corps were easy to get along with and friendly. My interest in shikar,

Author on joining – June 1956

which these friends shared, made it easier for me. It helped that I was able to enjoy dancing at the weekend club functions. Mhow had several ballroom dancing schools run by anglo-Indian families. Many of the girls were very good as partners and were most popular.

My father had gifted me an Indian Ordnance Factory made double barreled shotgun at the time of passing out. This enabled me to cycle out to some distance to shoot some partridge and sand grouse on weekends. A few of us would thus join each other on Sunday mornings. A few such officers, became life long friends.

On one such outing, near Akolia Rest House, I unwittingly stepped on to a mud coloured snake in the ploughed black-cotton-soil field. Luckily I had the deadly reptiles head just protruding from the side of the jungle boots I was wearing. I barely managed to jump clear and blow the snakes head off with the shotgun.

Mhow, had a fair amount of the painted partridges in the stretches of abundant grassland, which were used as ranges for the Infantry School. In the hedges and bushes and other scrub, there were some grey birds, that would flush out with a characteristic burst. We would cycle out on hired bikes, and get back by midday. More then once we came across a bunch of 'pardi' tribals who would be trapping game-birds with the use of dogs and nets. You could buy partrides and quails at the wayside Dhabas in those days.

Mhow was an old military garrison station, and had a fort, within which all the high explosive ammunition for the Infantry School was secured and stored. It had featured in the events of 1857. During World War II, it played a prominent part in the training of War time Emergency Commissioning of officers. In 1956, very scanty barracks and accommodation was available. Besides the Infantry School, the better organised Signals School was also co-located.

There were several field firing and other small arms classification ranges in the vicinity. 'Hema' was a flat grass covered

JOINING THE BATTALION

field firing range close by. 'Bercha' was another some distance away. It had an earthen bund forming an artificial lake. A large Banyan tree adjacent to the Bund gave the place its name . The far side of the lake, extending into the low hills around was notified as a field firing range. Bercha besides was a popular picnic spot, having a small rest house overlooking the lake on one side.

Mhow probably owes its name to the abundance of *Mahua* trees, scattered across the grass plains. During the British days, being close to Indore, the garrison perhaps kept a watchful eye on the Holkar rulers of the erstwhile princely state. It was the birth place of Dr Ambedkar, who had been born in a military family in Mhow. His contribution in the preparation of the Indian constitution makes him a legendary figure in India's preparation of an elaborate Constitution after freedom in 1947. The main road connecting the Capital at Delhi with Bombay, also passed through Indore and Mhow.

A year later I was back in the Infantry School to undergo training as a 3-inch mortar platoon commander. This time I had received proper pre-course training. I greatly enjoyed this opportunity at learning the handling of mortars as this was the most potent weapon in the infantry battalion. It is an un-caliberated weapon and is roughly aligned for the high trajectory bomb to land in the approximate target area. The bomb is cast iron one that breaks up into shrapnel to cause deadly affect.

During the final camp for firing at the Chhota Jam ranges, we learnt one evening of a leopard having killed a cow in a nearby village. Next evening some of us persisted and found the place where the kill had taken place. The villagers had set fire to the grass around the kill on the previous evening shortly after the kill had taken place. The killer had thus not been able to have a meal owing to the raging forest fire. We improvised a machan and sat up on the kill. The leopard turned up as expected after our waiting barely for an hour. I think he never even heard the shot that killed him.

We had a great camp fire and celebrations that night at the Chhota Jam camp..

Chhota Jam was an interesting Range as we fired the 3-Inch mortars from the edge of an escarpment onto lower ground almost a thousand feet below. The Malwa plateau abruptly falls away at the southern edge which gave us an interesting variation in controlling fire on targets below. Towards Mhow there is scattered grassland covering hills having some mixed jungle.

Dalbir, Kulwant Pannu, Self, Barar

SOME MORE SHIKAR EPISODES

KINWAT

(Kinwat was a very important and interesting experience for both of us brothers. Apart from the Shikar, it gave us an opportunity to briefly visit our father's ancestral roots from his mother's side. Kinwat was otherwise also a well recognized 'Shikar' area as I later learnt that Lt Gen S P Thorat and Air Chief Marshal Moolgaonkar had patronized it in their time)

My Battalion was still in the neighbourhood of Jammu at Ranbirsinghpura, facing the Pakistani deployment next to Sialkot at Suchetgarh in the summer of 1957. I was granted my first two month's annual leave in May and June. Lt Col Bolina, the CO, still seemed to bear a grudge over the 'cartoon' issue, and I had a difficult time explaining to the Second–in–Command (Major Nagarajan) that I had sought permission months in advance to enable Father to go ahead with the arrangements. After some time the CO relented, but left a sense of needless hurt in me. Father was still posted in Bombay and had made reservations to take both of us brothers on a big game shikar trip to Kinwat. Vijay was still at the National Defence Academy at Khadakvasla near Pune. His term break was to start a week later. He was to join us at Kinwat by train.

Kinwat Shooting Block was located in the Yeotmal district of Berar, and was not far from Father's ancestral village, Patur, near Akola. Besides, during the Hyderabad Police Action days, in 1948-50 he had been the Civil Administrator or Deputy Commissioner in Adilabad and then at Nanded in the adjoining area.

The metre-gauge line had since been extended in the years since the Police Action , connecting Nanded with Adilabad. Kinwat railway station was on this extended line. The Pain-Ganga River had formed the erstwhile boundary between Berar and Nizam's Hyderabad. Father, having spent several years earlier in these districts, had planned accordingly. Kinwat railway station on the southern side of the river got us to Kinwat Shooting Block, which was in the Yeotmal District, across and north of the river. Father had the necessary shooting block reservations done earlier from Bombay, where he was then posted.

Father and I travelled by train from Bombay to the shooting block and stayed at the comfortable Forest Rest House named after the block. We were received at the railway station by prior arrangement by some of Father's distant relatives, who had commandeered a pickup van for us. The van had a sturdy wooden *newar* bed tied on the superstructure. It enabled us to use it as a mobile *machan* - a useful innovation. The relatives who had come to help proved a great asset. Father was held in much regard at Patur, where he had spent many of his boyhood years.

After we settled down, we got going on the shikar routine to familiarize ourselves with the lie of the jungle. It initially meant a daily footslog of some miles. It being the hottest months of summer, the jungle was rather bare, but it was helpful as the tigers were expected to be confined to places having some residual pools of water.

The local guide and Shikari, named Rainba, took matters in hand and selected the sites for tie-up of baits at some select spots. One of the very promising bait tie-up spots was in a densely

wooded nala named *'Baghbooda'*. It was known watering hole for tigers in the seclusion of some thick bamboo jungle. A small pool of stagnant water survived the summer heat. *'Baghbooda'* in Marathi means, the place where tigers were known to immerse themselves in the pool of water in the summer months. Tigers are well known to be doing this to overcome the summer heat. The same nala drained into the Pain-Ganga river further downstream.

Rainba was a little more than 50 years old at that time. As his photograph shows, he was already aging prematurely. He was having trouble with his eyesight. Having been at Kinwat for long years, he was full of stories of the past. A British Army officer had been severely mauled in one of these episodes by a wounded tiger, many years before. Father's ability to speak fluently in Marathi, quickly drew Rainba out.

Rainba took us to *Baghbooda* nala the very next day. A male buffalo calf was to be tied up at this spot as the bait. We had driven to the place by the forest road in the van, which got us fairly close to the site. The baits were to be tied as a regular routine at two other places besides the *Baghbooda* nala. However, from the beginning, Rainba seemed most hopeful of success at this site.

Next morning we visited the sites where the baits had been tied up on the first night of our stay. None of the baits had been taken. However, while visiting the *Baghbooda* site, Father had a brainwave and suggested that a path be swept of all leaves to enable us to get quietly to a spot from where we could view the bait from a hidden spot from about 75 yards downstream of the dry nala. This would enable us to view the

1957 – Kinwat – Rainba the Shikari

bait surreptitiously without getting too close to it. Accordingly, a path was swept in such a manner that it enabled us to view the bait from some distance. The bamboo jungle around the view point completely hid the place, if you carefully used the swept path. It meant you could get to view the bait without disturbing the site. Using rubber jungle boots or bare feet, this innovation of a silent approach proved very useful.

Two days later, as we left the van on the forest road and were still some distance from where the bait was tied up next to the shallow pool of water, a peafowl gave out a loud alarm call of '*khok* – khok –khok' and took flight with a noisy flapping of wings. This un-mistaken jungle sign from the vicinity of where the bait was tied was a definite indicator that a tiger had possibly made a kill and was still in the area where the bait was located.

We stopped breathlessly and checked the weapons for being loaded and ready. I was carrying the . 30-06 Mauser and Father was carrying his trusted . 405 Winchester Rifle.

I led the way silently, using the swept way to the vantage point from where the bait could be secretly viewed . As I quietly settled down and took a look around, I could see that the bait had been killed and the tiger had eaten a substantial meal. Even from that distance, I could see the red flesh and bones of the dead bait which lay exposed. The tiger had after his meal moved away and was itself not visible near the kill. The tiger was apparently somewhere in the vicinity as the peafowl had warned. Father and some others including Rainba also crept up one by one and joined me as I scanned the area. The noiseless approach had paid off so far. The screen of bamboo fronds covered us in the light and shade.

The Tiger's Kill

All of us quietly looked on towards the dead bait. Then quite unexpectedly, I saw the tiger moving in the tall grass on the far side opposite us across the dry water course. Quite unaware of us, the tiger slowly turned around and ambled slowly back to where the kill lay. The tiger had been much closer to us than expected, and our luck was holding that he had not detected us. As the tiger got close to the dead bait, he stood looking down at the kill. My shot caught him in the neck. He rose up on his hind legs and fell full length backwards. His tail thrashed a couple of times in the death throes and he thereafter lay still. When we got to him a little later, he seemed fast asleep on the carpet of dry bamboo leaves.

Baghbooda Tiger – As he Fell

To a twenty something year old, it was a crowning moment and achievement for me. It was owed almost entirely to Deva-Pitta's forethought of having the path swept that allowed us to get such an opportunity. The tiger was a male and was 9 feet and 8 inches between pegs. Shooting a tiger, was in those days considered an important Shikar event. Having done so from the ground on the very first opportunity, I felt most elated.

I later realized that I had used a light .30-06 Mauser rifle. The 120 grain bullet was rather light for a tiger and the shot having proved fatal by breaking the neck of the animal was a stroke of luck. Father's .405 Winchester, using a 300 grain bullet, would have been the more appropriate weapon. This did not occur to me at that time. Beginners luck!

Wily Rainba had looked around and came up with the startling news that from the pug marks, it appeared that there had also been a tigress around. From the amount of flesh that had been

eaten, it appeared he may be right. Since the shooting permit only allowed for "a tiger" in the Kinwat Block, Father suggested that I sit up over the kill and treat the occasion to gain some experience. I was not to shoot if the second tiger showed up.

I got back later that afternoon after attending to the skinning of the tiger. It was a hot May afternoon and I dozed off on the machan that had been put up. As I settled down, I also became aware of several nests of red ants around the machan. I was a little wary of this as red ants have a potent sting. Mercifully, as the evening cooled down the agitated ants settled down for the night.

Nothing significant happened except I distinctly heard a tiger call once from not too far away. Perhaps the excessive disturbance in the area of the kill during the day, did not allow the second tiger to come to the kill.

*****

Rainba the Shikari had mentioned that almost all the small hamlets and small villages in the area were surrounded with bare, black cotton soil fields. Most such villages had leopards, invariably sneaking around at night to pick up the village dogs or stray cattle.

Some two days later, we drove several miles to where the Forest Office was located to partake of an evening meal with the Forest Range Officer on his invitation. He had a pleasant and polished personality and resembled Balraj Sahni, the film actor. We used the pickup van which had the inverted '*newar*' bed tied up on the superstructure, which made it a 'mobile *machan*,' and was a great help. It allowed you the advantage of some height and it was not unpleasant with the summer's evening breeze.

I had clamped a three cell torch onto the Mauser.30.06 Rifle, which I was carrying as we drove off for the evening to the Range Officer's place. Most of the forest road was through mixed teak forest. The jungle was quite bare as the teak had shed the broad

leaves during the summer months. Enroute we passed a small hamlet which was surrounded by bare black soil fields. The jungle was some distance away from the village and as the pickup van drove past the cluster of huts, we saw a jackal cross the road ahead of us as the headlights of the vehicle reached it. The jackal kept looking back at something that seemed to be bothering him.

Mobile Machine

We had a spotlight attached to the vans battery, which could only be used sparingly as the car's battery could not take the extra load. I asked the person holding the spotlight to switch the light on and see what was bothering the jackal. As the light came on, it fell upon and lit up a leopard, which was thus caught in the open and clearly visible against the black cotton soil.

The leopard was in the vicinity of village huts, looking to pick up stay dogs or any cattle by chance . As the light fell on him, he uneasily shifted backwards to make a quick getaway to the jungle which was several hundred yards away. He started to move briskly away to cross the forest road to make a getaway.

The pickup van driver and his companion in the cab too had also seen the leopard caught in the patch of light. The driver seemed to get a bit excited and a faulty clutch release managed to have the vehicle engine stall and then go off. We were suddenly plunged into darkness. The already weak battery could not sustain the load of the headlights and the spotlight. With nail-biting tension, we waited for the vehicle to be crank started.

Meanwhile the leopard was briskly making his way to the nearest jungle. As the battery could not be used for the self-starter, there ensued a period of uncertainty as someone had to get down and hand crank the vehicle to get it started. It took a few minutes of tense waiting as the person in the cab bravely got down and cranked the engine to life. We all sat through the anxious few minutes in the total darkness. The three-cell torch attached to the Mauser rifle was quite unable to light up the leopard as he was yet some distance away, rapidly making good his escape. As the engine started up the vehicle moved rapidly reducing the distance to where the leopard had already crossed the road on his way to the jungle edge which was still about 200 yards away from him. With his ears laid back he was hurrying along and I realized that he would soon be safely away if I did not take a shot in the next few seconds.

Someone commented that a chance had been lost. As I heard the remark I switched on the torch light to illuminate the rifle's foresight. Aiming for the base of the leopard's tail, I chanced the shot at the rapidly receding target. The leopard seem to wobble on receiving the shot and raising some dust, dashed away as I took another hasty and somewhat desperate shot. The pickup van driver had taken his eyes of the road again to see what was happening, which resulted in the vehicle engine stalling yet again and bringing us to a sudden stop. The headlights and the spotlight went off, leaving us in complete darkness at the very moment we needed it most. The leopard had just disappeared in the darkness.

The torch light from the torch clamped onto the rifle could not penetrate the gloom and dust raised by the vehicle.

After some confusion, the pickup van was again crank started, and the spotlight was re-activated. It revealed nothing as the leopard seemed to have just vanished into thin air. The ground sloped gently up towards the edge of the jungle, and the leopard seemed to have covered the distance during the period of confusion over the re-starting of the vehicle.

We spent some time probing the area with the searchlight, but there was no trace of the leopard. We even turned the pickup van in that direction to flood the area with light, but discovered a trench like drain that impeded our going further.

So, after a suitable period we proceeded for our evening engagement for dinner with the range officer. The banter in the party with us were sceptical and felt that the chance had been missed. Only Rainba, the old local shikari, expressed the opinion that the leopard was definitely hit at the base of the tail. The shot would have raked the animal from end to end, causing it a fatal injury.

On our way back from the dinner engagement, the driver stopped the vehicle at the spot where the leopard had crossed over the road earlier in the evening. On systematically searching the ground now, we found that the leopard's face and head was just visible as a faint blur. He had been unable to reach the jungle and had taken refuge in a slight fold in the ground. His one eye reflected the light and it seemed the stricken animal had indeed been very hard hit as Rainba had assessed. He had taken shelter in a slight fold in the ground.

Now it was a very difficult target at a considerable range. Father also advised that the injured animal should be put out of the misery he seemed to be in. The foresight of the rifle seemed to cover the blurred target. At my chancing the shot, the visible target just disappeared from view.

Early next morning when we got there, we found the leopard dead. The first shot had raked forward from the base of the tail, causing grievous injury. The second shot taken hastily immediately after the first, had been a clean miss. But the third shot taken during our return journey at the barely visible head had proved fatal as it had struck the animal in the throat. A sheer fluke is all that I can call that.

*****

Father arranged with the Forest Department for the allotment of another neighboring block. My younger brother Vijay, joined us for his summer break from the National Defence Academy at Khadakvasla, where he was then. We accordingly moved to a small Forest Department Inspection hut at a place called Korat, more central to the block now allotted for my brother. Father, meanwhile had a couple of days official commitment of work at the state capital of Hyderabad. He was then Regional Resettlement Commissioner for Central, Western and South India at that time. He was located at Bombay (Mumbai). He had a lot of touring to do over the vast area allotted to him.

Brother Vijay arrived by train at the Kinwat Station and Father left for the work he had at Hyderabad. He would rejoin us after a few days. We moved our camp to Korat forest department inspection hut. Rainba our Shikari guide and jungle mentor took stock of the new area. We were busy cleaning and oiling the weapons, and generally taking it 'easy' at the changed location on the first day.

By early midday Rainba rushed in with the news that a tiger had just killed a cow in broad daylight from the village cattle herd. The place where this had happened was a few miles from where we were. We immediately got organized to take advantage of this unexpected good news.

We got to the general area quickly, using the pickup van for covering most of the distance. The villager whose cow had

been killed led the way. We silently stalked to where we found the tiger had been lying in a cool patch of water in the shady nala. The tiger had just left the pool as his pug marks were so fresh and were only just filling in with water seeping in. Rainba with caution led us further as we followed the rapidly drying pugmarks.

As we cautiously moved forward, Rainba whispered that the big male tiger may possibly suddenly charge us to show his possession of the kill. Vijay and I exchanged anxious looks. Vijay was using Father's .405 Winchester Rifle while I had the .30-06 Mauser, a much lighter weapon in a supporting role. Being the elder of the two I could have been more careful, but opted to keep going. A somewhat rash decision taken in some haste, and in hindsight, attributable to inexperience of youth. Luckily we got away with it.

The villager who had lost his cow to the tiger had barely climbed a tree for a couple of feet, when he nearly fell back on top of us on sighting the tiger in the deep shadow of a *Mahua* tree located about 80 yards or so from us. The tiger had seen the man climb the tree and shortly thereafter, I clearly saw the tiger, a long red streak of him, rushing away to a flank. The glare of the summer day's brightness of the sun, contrasted with the deep shadow of the *Mahua* tree under which the tiger had been resting until we disturbed him. The cow killed by him lay in the sun a few paces away.

Rainba had urgently whispered earlier, that the tiger having made a "natural" kill could be very possessive of it and could have demonstrated angrily at our intrusion. Luckily for us, he had opted out of a confrontation. His pug marks showed him to be a oversized male. Rainba said the tiger was likely to remain in the vicinity to claim his kill.

While we waited quietly under the *Mahua* tree, a couple of accompanying men went back to the village to get things for

putting up a machan. They returned within the hour, using the pickup van. A machan was put up silently and Vijay and I took up our place on it by mid-afternoon.

Here, I made a mistake by insisting on changing the position of the dead cow by a couple of yards. Rainba cautioned that the tiger was a wily old campaigner, and would be most suspicious of any tampering with the kill.

Sure enough the tiger seems to have followed Rainba and the villagers to where they were to wait near the pickup van. The tiger then came back, stalking the kill, following the route we had taken in approaching. Vijay clearly saw him looking suspiciously at the kill from a distance. The wily animal, noticing the changed position of the dead cow and just melted away into the jungle. Rainba had been right, as we never saw anything of him thereafter. We sat up that night and the next and drew a total blank. A lesson learnt that you cannot underestimate the natural instinct of survival of the great cats.

We seemed to run out of luck thereafter. There was an equally wily leopard around Korat who managed to keep out of harms way. We would see his eyes glowing in the distance, but he would dodge away when we tried getting closer.

Deva-Pitta returned after his brief trip to Hyderabad. We stayed a few more days but we had no further luck. Father decided to round off the trip by taking us brothers to his ancestral village, Patur, in the close proximity of the district town of Akola in Berar. It was a unique opportunity for both of us.

The Kinwat trip was a unique one as it was in the close vicinity of the place where I had bagged my first panther many years before in the Adilabad District. Rainba, the very experienced jungle craftsman, was full of wise council and advise. He was already in his fifties and full of stories of shikar in the days gone by. He had accompanied many sportsmen in the colonial days, and knew every inch of the jungle.

Rainba narrated how he once was secretly taking a look at a tigress's cubs in a dry nala when she attacked and knocked him over. What saved him was that she knocked his pagri off and began roughing that up while Rainba managed to get away by climbing a nearby tree.

*****

Our visit to the ancestral village was too fleeting to leave much of an impression. In later years Father, would nostalgically remember his childhood spent at Patur, his mother's side of the past. Later, when he retired from government service and settled down at Dehradun, he named his place in Clement Town as 'Patur'. In 1990 on my suggestion, he wrote a few paragraphs about the past and Patur, which I am giving below.

" ....the progeny of the warrior clan to which my ancestors belonged claimed direct descent from the Sun or Moon God. Some of these fighting men who came down South with the invading Mughal armies, indeed became a part of a lesser nobility, by becoming 'Mansabdars' of the local satrap (Nizam of Hyderabad). The latter's lien of a Jagir village, expected them to produce a set number of foot and horse soldiers ,in times of war, even bullock carts and camels to transport commissariat".

"In peacetime, the Mansabdar was expected to pay an annual visit to Hyderabad, to pay obeisance to the Nizam, ruler of the Deccan."

"On one such visit the old Mansabdar failed to return from the annual visit to Hyderabad and 'Tara,' the beautiful female riding elephant, just pined away and starved to death on hearing the Mahout say –'master has passed away' "

"The Jagir village belonging to our branch of the family, called Chili, was located on the outskirt of Berar (the part of the Nizam's dominion ceded to the British), near the Pen-Ganga river

which separated Berar from the rest of Hyderabad (territory). A somewhat Godforsaken place, subject to dacoities from across the River".

"Once at ancestral village Chilli, the dacoits took it into their heads to rob the rich jagirdar. They surrounded his 'Haveli' after dark and after firing some threatening rounds in the air, shouted to our ancestor to surrender all his cash and gold meekly. The wily old Rajput thought of a stratagem. He offered to hand over all his valuables to the gangster at the small opening in the big gate of the ' Haveli.' But as the leading dacoit put his arm inside the small opening to pick up the booty, the master of the 'Haveli' just severed the outstretched arm with a single stroke of his mighty sword. The opening was quickly shut and chained but it was of no avail as the infuriated dacoits set the big Haveli on fire.

Obviously, for the inmates the time had come to repeat the age old chivalry of the Rajputs, where the men went out to fight the enemy, and the women of the house prepared for the time-honoured immolation to save their honour, the customary 'jauhar'. In this case the women were asked to crowd themselves into some big inverted old iron cauldrons or 'karais' and await the end without emitting a sound from their concealment under those huge iron contraptions. While the men went out and killed and got killed, the poor women were just roasted alive in the inferno under those iron 'karhais'."

"After this sad event such as my ancestors who happened to be away at the time of this tragic event and had survived thought it wiser to move away to a safer place far from the border.They left the Jagir and all it had to the management of a 'Karbhari' (Manager) and they moved to Patur."

" Grandpa, my mother's father, was a very unusual man. With his Jagir village and some 50 odd acres of land in Patur, he did not have to work for a living. But he spent recklessly throughout his life, not on himself, but mostly on others: on helping the poorest

of the poor and the downtrodden. The result, after his passing away, Grandma (Ammaji) found herself heavily in debt and was obliged to sell the dear Jagir old family village Chilli for just a pittance......."

"Grandma's (Ammaji's) people, being of similar descent were also soldiers. She hailed from Wasim, some 30 miles away from Patur. Her father, a horse soldier, had been a Risaldar in the Nizam's forces, was a member of the first contingent of Indian forces ever to cross the wide seas when the all powerful European nations ,decided to invade China; the Sleeping Giant. A contingent of Indian State Forces, led by Maharaja Sir Pratap Singh of Jodhpur, formed part of the British forces, in the notorious Opium War (1840- 42). The hapless Chinese fled before the mounted lancers and there was a lot of general stampede, massacre and looting. Granny's father returned home with his share of booty. However, easy come easy go, Granny who brought some of this precious jewellery as apart of her dowry , was soon deprived of most of it by an unscrupulous brother who thought nothing of a trusting sister's confidence".

"Grandpa Shiv Ratan Singh Verma, popularly called 'Daadoo' for his fartherly ways, was a most unusual and atypical Indian for his days, at the beginning of the 20th Century. Being an innovator, he was the first to bring potato, kerosene oil, and a lantern to our village. He started a boys' middle school and a girls' primary school in the village. The former has blossomed into a college – and still preserves a stone bust with some likeness of the bearded old Rajput with a bulging pugri, respectfully installed by a grateful people in the Assembly Hall. He also persuaded the authorities to start a dispensary with a doctor in our village......."

THE SHIMLA HILLS — SABATHU

The Battalion's next station was in the Shimla Hills. Sabathu was a quaint, one-battalion station. It had been largely used in the past in the days of the Raj for British units as it gave them some respite from the summer heat in the plains. Sabathu, was a 'stop-over' place in the early days for the Governor-General's entourage during his move to Shimla. The bridle route used for tongas, palanquins and horses was still discernable at places, as it connected with Solan for onward move to Shimla. The construction of the railway and the main road had changed things for good.

We replaced an Assam Regiment battalion. I noticed that the Red Faced monkeys (Rhesus Macaqe, Macaca mulatta), the few that one got to see in the jungle around Sabathu, were very wary of the men in olive green uniform. Some of the tribals in the Assam Regiment probably were fond of monkey meat. That probably explained the unusual shyness of the monkeys in the jungle around Sabathu. Usually, these primates become a considerable nuisance in big cities, boldly moving around human habitation. They do a lot of damage and are a pest that is very difficult to control.

The history of Sabathu was that during the early 19th Century, it was used as the controlling place or headquarters by the Gorkhas earlier in their conquest of the area. The name 'Sabathu' was formed by merging two words, 'Suba'and 'Taur'.The Battle at 'Malaun' in 1805 between the Gorkhas and the British, midway towards where Shimla came up later, led to the absorption of these hill men into the British – Indian Army. 1st Gurkha Rifles was raised here thereafter. It was a noteworthy aspect of their expansion in the subcontinent, that they absorbed those that had fought well against them into their own led Indian Army. Gurkha Rifles and The Sikh Regiment were thus raised.

After our tenure, Sabathu was rightly made the 1st and- 4th Gorkha Centre (14 GTC , please note the British spelling of 'Gurkha' and our 'Gorkha', post 1947). The Gorkha Fort ruins on prominent hill tops are still visible at many scattered places in the Kangra Valley and other parts of Himachal Pradeshs even today.

Our Hill brigade formed a part of 4 Infantry Division, its other formations located mainly around Ambala. We formed part of 11 Brigade (the Hill Brigade), which had its Headquarters at Kasauli and its other two infantry battalions at Dagshai. Our stay at our idyllic station was disturbed when we were moved down to Ambala, to join in the unpleasant Operation 'AMAR' in providing troop labour for constructing married accommodation. Major General B M Kaul, our General Officer Commanding (GOC), was out to make his 'mark' with Krishna Menon and Prime Minister Nehru at the expense of troops being used thus. Living under canvas for long periods was most unpopular with the rank and file.

The battalion got a new CO when Lt Col Maha Singh Rikh took over from Lt Col Bolina. He had been an instructor in the 'Junior Commander Wing' (JC Course) before coming to us as Second-in-Command for a few months, prior to taking over Command of the Unit. He was from a *'talukdar'* Christian family of well- to- do land-owners of Bijnore. His place was called *'Raja –ka-Tajpur'*. He had earlier served in the 3rd Battalion. He had married his own widowed aunt – a tall anglo-Indian lady named Molly, who had two grown sons from her previous marriage. She also had a high-strung Lhasa Apso, named 'Tipsy', whose set back lower under-slung jaw and his beady shining eyes half covered by a fringe of hair gave him an unfriendly look. He behaved as if he knew he was the CO's dog. Having only a little stump for a tail he conveyed his pleasure by flexing his ears.

Colonel Rikh took over just prior to our unwelcome move to Ambala for Op AMAR. Just when the Battalion was looking forward to a happy tenure at the small station of Sabathu, with most of our officers families having just joined, an extended stay under tentage at Ambala was not popular.

Further, we had a sad setback at Ambala, when 2/lt Ragunath Jaswal, the next senior to me – died in the Ambala Military Hospital. A military funeral is a very moving and sad event. Jaswal's baby daughter Sujata, clinging to the beads around her mothers neck, as Shree Ram the Bugler, sounded the Last Post. It remains one of the saddest moments of one's life. Ragunath came down with stomach cramps after a strenuous game of hockey. He developed a serious 'intestinal blockage' that the hospital could not overcome. His loss was greatly felt by us, the younger lot. Being from the ranks he was several years older than us and had married Krishna, the daughter of a retired Honarary Captain of The Dogra Regiment settled near Garh Shankar, close to Hoshiarpur.

The Battalion moved back from Ambala after completion of the task. Prime Minister Nehru, accompanied by Defence Minister Krishna Menon, attended an official '**Bara Khana**' after the inaugural ceremony at Ambala. Even the Mess silver trophies were brought down from Sabathu and displayed 'on orders'. General K S Thimmaya, the then Chief, was also a silent spectator of the goings on.

ROMANCE AND MARRIAGE

During December 1958, I accompanied Father and elder sister Meera to attend younger brother Vijay's Passing Out Parade at the Indian Military Academy at Dehradun. We stayed with the Hoons in their place on Balbir Road, in Dalanwala. Their son Sudhir was also passing out at the same parade. Sudhir had lost about a year having tried his hand at 'flying'. Sudhir was being commissioned into the Armoured Corps, where he was later to be popularly called 'Marshal'. Younger brother Vijay had opted for my Regiment, The Rajputs –and was to go to The 14th Battalion which was then in the operationally active Naga Hills.

Mr. H S Hoon and Mrs Saraswati Hoon were old-time family acquaintances. We had stayed with Saraswati's elder sister (Vidyawati), wife of Rai Bahadur Swami Das at Lahore in 1942 during our trip to Kashmir. Both the sisters lived in the same neighborhood in adjacent bunglows in Model Town in Lahore. They had both been at Kanya Maha Vidalaya during my great-grandmother's time there. Ammaji, our great-grand mother, was held in great esteem in the Punjab of those days for her role in the premier women's college at Jalandhar. After partition the Hoons managed to find a place on Balbir Avenue in Dalanwala, Dehradun. The house had an unusual layout of a widely separated 'Zenana' from a detached drawing room, with an enclosed courtyard separating the two.

ROMANCE AND MARRIAGE

Father had always kept in touch with the extended Hoon family owing to the Jalandhar Kanya Mahavidyalayai connection. The Hoons had been uprooted from their home in Model Town at Lahore during partition. However, the family members struggled hard to overcome the shattering blow they had suffered during partition. Deva-Pitta was always treated with great regard by the Hoon family over the years. It was natural that we were welcomed with great warmth when we were visiting Dehradun for Vijay's passing out from the Academy. Both my parents had been treated with great affection during their sojourn in London and Europe during 1958 with one of their sons, settled there.

Perhaps a tentative matrimonial proposal had been aired during the London stay but during that evening in Dehradun, I could sense that something like a marriage proposal was brewing for their daughter Usha and me . When we left for the parade at the Academy, I was driving Sister Meera's Austin A 40 car, and noticed being closely observed from the rear seat by the young lady wearing a pink sari and a black coat. Her dark glasses could not quite conceal her watching me closely in the rear view mirror. After the parade I got the opportunity to show her a medal that one of the passing out Gentlemen Cadet had been awarded.

Later, when driving back to Ambala Father broached the subject with me. Madhu Seth, sister Meera's husband, was commanding an Artillery unit in Ambala, felt that I was too young at 23 years age to get settled in a marriage. He accordingly advised against a hasty decision in this regard. He also mentioned that Regulations for the Army frowned upon officers marrying before a certain age.

December 1958: (from left to right) Mr H.S. Hoon, Meera,
Mrs Hoon, Usha and Father
(Standing) Sudhir Hoon, Brijesh Guleria, Vijay and Self

At Ambala the Battalion was still there, winding up after Op AMAR, I sought the CO's (Col Rikh), guidance in the matter, fully expecting a curt rebuff. Taking me quite by surprise, without a moments hesitation, he favoured the proposal. He said the Battalion still had two years at Sabathu and we could make the best of it as a 'family station'. The CO's advice took me a bit by surprise. He said that a happy marriage can make or mar an officer's life in the Infantry. Since the proposal for my settling down seemed from a known family, he felt I should take the plunge. He said that he would support the proposal wholeheartedly. Coming from him, who had been a bachelor most of his life, his spontaneous advice made a lot of sense to me.

That night when I went to see off father at the Ambala Cantonment Railway Station, I told him of my acceptance of the

ROMANCE AND MARRIAGE

idea of settling down early. He seemed a bit amused but happy. This led to elder sister Meera accompanying me to Dehradun for a brief engagement ceremony in March 1959. We were to be married on June 11th. Father wrote to the Hoons accordingly, He also wrote to Usha (he had met her several times before at Madras where she was in college) that I was quite smitten and bowled over on having met her during the Dehradun visit.

Back at Sabathu, the unit having moved back, we got back to the routine training. It was a happy period for all of us in the family station. I was made the understudy Quarter-Master (QM) of the battalion. Major Bramanand Awasty, a senior World War veteran was to teach me the basics of logistics of the unit. He was good at handling 'anything' in the battalion, and I soon realized how useful it was to learn things from him. Awasthy was already reputed to be perhaps the best officer in the whole Rajput Regiment at that time. An excellent hockey player, he had just returned from Gurdaspur where he had been a 'Brigade Major, a most prestigious appointment. He was quite the role model for us youngsters. Being his understudy was a unique privilege for me.

Major Awasthy once told me that unlike the adjutant, who is the 'Right Hand' man of the CO, the QM is the one who keeps the men fed and clothed. It is the QM who makes sure hot tea and meals are provided at the right time and place. Less glamorous, you are left a great deal to do your own bit – if you have it in you. Care and upkeep of the weapons and regular inspections was also included in the charter of duties. I found that under his guidance, I was enjoying the QM's job

At Sabathu, apart from exchanging a few awkward letters with Usha, I began to realised that perhaps I could boldly breathe some romance into the proposal. I had hardly even spoken to my fiancée. I decided that I would pay a surprise visit to the Hoons at Dehradun. With that in mind I managed to borrow an old ex-Army disposal 'Matchless' motorcycle for the proposed trip to Dehradun

from Captain Partojit Choudhry of 1/9 Gorkha Rifles. Parto and I would often spend the weekends together trying to shoot some black hill partridges and Kaleej Pheasants in the wooded nalas in the area. He would drive down on his 'Matchless' motorcycle from Dagshai where his battalion was located. Parto was a Sword of Honour winner, from a course a year senior to me, and a very pleasant and likeable person. He had a million dollar smile that lit up sometimes when we were together. He readily loaned me his motorcycle with the remark that I should have it checked out for the trip to Dehradun.

'MATCHLESS' TRIP

Partojit's Matchless motorcycle had been acquired by him from the 'Army's Disposals'. The Army was still using the Matchless machines, so spares were commonly available. I requested Havildar Pritam Ram, the burly, Gujar MT (Mechanical Transport) Havildar to please check out on Partojit's machine for its road worthiness. Pritam brought the machine back the next day, pronouncing it 'fit' for the trip. He, however, then told me that five out of the six wheel nuts had been missing, which he had replaced. He also showed me how the petrol tank had been firmly secured with fresh screws and nuts. The headlights though, were barely functional.

Taking a few days' casual leave, with some clothes in a kit-bag tied behind, and some *chutney* sandwiches, I took off. The route I followed was via Dharampur, from where I followed the main road going to Shimla over a short distance past Dagshai, to a lesser, known tarred hill road branching off to Nahan. The route was through beautiful pine jungle, and I came across no traffic enroute. A brief stop at Nahan for a tea break, then I started off for Poanta. The beautiful sal forest made the drive very pleasant but I knew that I had to hurry to catch the Rampur-Mandi ferry on the Jamuna river. I got to the ferry just as they were closing down that evening. They proved helpful and got me across just as it was getting late in the evening. I barely got to Herbertpur when I realized that the petrol tank between my knees was nearly empty. It was already dark, but fortunately I managed to get some petrol from a Sikh Dhabawala who had some to spare.

Fortunately it was a moonlit night and the trip from Herbertpur to Dehradun went off without a hitch. I could only use the headlight very sparingly. Imagine my feeling on getting to the Hoon's house on Balbir Road, to find a big padlock on the door leading into the enclosed courtyard of the house. For a few minutes I did not know what to make of the situation or what I could do at that late hour. I moved back from the padlocked door to where the 'Matchless' was parked. When I looked back again towards the house I then noticed that some lights were still on in the inner portion of the house. I also detected even a radio was playing a popular hindi movie song within those inner rooms.

Usha's father had been a policeman in the pre-partition days in Punjab, and his fetish for security, would lead to locking himself and the family up safely at night. With some persistent knocking, Mr. Hoon opened the door only to disappoint me with the news that Usha and her mother and younger sister had gone to Delhi for the preparatory shopping for the wedding. Somewhat disappointed, I finally got to eat the sandwiches before getting some sleep.

Mr. Hoon had lost an eye in a cataract operation and the scrutiny that he subjected me to with his good eye the next morning when he questioned me as to who I was and why I was there, deflated me quite a bit. He had let me in the night before, still holding his policeman's stout cane 'danda' in his hand. He was more helpful, when I told him that I intended going on to Delhi. Still a little hesitant, he gave me the Karol Bagh Address of Chandrawali 'Aunty' with whom Mrs Hoon and the girls were staying.

Finally, with bloodshot eyes after the drive to Delhi, I managed to locate Usha, her mother and younger sister Sudha at Chandrawali Aunty's. I still had a couple days of leave left,

so I did my best to make the best of the surprise I had been able to spring. I found that a couple of drops of 'rose-water' are very soothening for the bloodshot eyes. I think I managed to begin a lifelong friendship with her during this trip.

When I got back to Sabathu, using the direct road leading to Shimla, I sent for Havildar Pritam Ram of the MT to checkout on the 'Matchless' before returning it to Partojit. He came back with the report that several of the five wheel nuts he had replaced had fallen out again during the trip.

It is now almost sixty years when I undertook that escapade through jungle covered distances. That I could pull it off means I had some kind of divine help always – when I needed it.

MARRIAGE AND AFTER

We got back to Ambala after the wedding, enroute to Sabathu. Elder sister Meera's husband was commanding an Artillery Regiment and had a spacious bungalow in the Cantonment. We stopped over at Ambala for a couple of days.

We were to be married on the premises of the Doon School, which was having its summer break. Usha's uncle, Mr. Viswanath Kapoor was House Master of Jaipur House and the groom's party were housed in the vacant students dormitory. The ceremony was held at the Holding House Annex, just across the road leading into the cantonment. Colonel Rikh and all the officers of the Battalion attended, leaving just one Duty officer behind at Sabathu. This had been done with the permission of Brigadier Bhagwati Singh, our Brigade Commander at Kasauli. It was an singular honour having all the officers attending the function . Even Captain Seetaraman, the doctor, attended. Captain Kulwant Pannu drove all the way on a scooter from Agra to attend. He had transferred from the Dogra Regiment and was with 2 PARA in the Parachute Brigade.

Kulwant Pannu was a big hearted friend several years my senior. We were to meet many years later in Dhaka, he after his dramatic drop at Tangail with 2 Para (*In the War for the liberation of Bangladesh, 2 Para was dropped North of Dhaka on 11 December 1971*). We were both commanding our respective battalions in the War for the Liberation of Bangladesh. I had foot-slogged all the way from Agartala. They had just announced his Maha Vir Chakra, and

MARRIAGE AND AFTER

I pulled his leg for once having "jumped to Conclusion" correctly.

Being the leechi ripening season, the Jaipur House fruit trees were laden with succulent red fruit bunches, which I could reach mounted on a brown horse, had me tossing bunches to all and sundry before moving over for the ceremony to Holding House. Ours was a simple enough ceremony with minimum fuss. After the ceremony I got back to the dormitory and slept on a bare newar bed after pushing brother Vijay's black spaniel 'Lady' off. None of that '*Suhag Raat*' crap that you see in the Television Serials these days. Frankly, I didn't know better at that time.

On getting back to Sabathu, the CO, Colonel Rikh, met us a few miles outside the place and drove us into the cantonment in his jeep. It was a bit embarrassing to be accorded such a welcome for us. Usually, officers get married whilst on leave and the newly weds are given a reception at the officers Mess. In my case the CO turned it into a 'Regimental Event', which bowled us over. Few, if any get this kind of reception, that we got. After the cut and dried approach of Lt Col H S Bolina, the previous CO, Lt Col Maha Singh Rikh's handling of us was completely different.

Usha and I set up home in a yellow house on a hilltop on the western edge of Sabathu. The house provided a bird eye view with the Officers Mess on an adjacent spur, the CO's bungalow further away, and a small church on top of the knoll. However, the most central feature of Sabathu was the large Parade ground. The barracks and offices were on the rising hill beyond the parade ground. There was also a small civilian bazaar tucked away to a defladed flank. The bachelors stayed in a white bungalow next to the Mess named 'Silverton'. Sabathu was a real 'one horse' town and even electricity had only recently been installed.

During the latter half of September, Army Chief General Thimaya, during a visit to Kasauli at the Brigade Headquarters, addressed all the officers of the formation. The incident of his spat with Krishna Menon, the Defence Minister, had only recently taken place, and we were all aware of it generally. The General was rather subdued and not his sparkling self during the talk. He told us of the problem that was brewing against the Chinese, in particular about the deployment of our division (4 Infantry Division) by the year end in North-Eastern India. We for the first time heard of NEFA, the North East Frontier Agency.

TRAIN TO THE NORTH – EAST

The Quartermaster of an infantry battalion has a lot to do at the time of such a move. We had to close down at Sabathu, handing over all the accommodation and other assets to the troublesome MES staff (Military Engineering Service). Next, a move down to Kalka for the whole unit in such a manner that boarding the train was carried out in one continuous flow. It all went off without a serious mishap or hitch, and finally the evening meal being served on the platform for the men. However, a stage came when it seemed like a breakdown in all semblance of all 'military order'. I gave up and retreated to the waiting room and put my feet up on that colonial invention, the easy chair with leg rests. All the Units baggage had already been loaded in daylight in covered wagons. When I stepped out of the waiting room a little later, it all looked as tidy and orderly as I had wanted it to be.

Finally, the CO and all the other officers arrived and occupied their allotted accommodations. The Battalion's Band played the last tune and Band Major Shiv Singh reported to the Adjutant. The train was at last cleared for the long move to the North East by the railway staff. Demand for milk and meat had already been initiated for the stations enroute. Train halts were worked out for some physical activity and meals. Bugle calls were used and the organized journey trip got underway. Families had dispersed earlier.

In those days there was a major problem changing to a metre-guage train at Mukamah in Bihar. It was a nightmarish task as the capacity of metre-gauge wagons was quite different from the broad gauge. I was careful in making sure that the unit's ammunition wagons were marked accordingly with chalk in my own handwriting. Since several other units had moved before us the marking with chalk were at best very confusing. It was lucky we had done this as at our Siliguri station halt, we had red smoke emitting from a wagon, which had "ammunition" written in chalk. I quickly recognized the problem as the Armourer's Stores in the wagon had a large bottle of nitric acid in it. We could thus dispose of the problem speedily. Lesson learnt was that such sensitive stores must be disposed off before undertaking such a journey.

The officers quite enjoyed the train trip. Interconnected with telephones, a lot of beer and bridge sessions enabled us to pass time. Gradually the terrain changed and gave way to intermittent thick jungle and tea gardens of Assam. Our destination was a sleepy station named Rangapara-North. Our advance party had done the needful and we detrained from the train after almost a week's journey from Kalka. We were told that the Forest Department had permitted our cutting of sufficient bamboo and grass to make our own hutted accommodation at a place near Lokhra. Initially using tentage, we got going on the task of setting up a camp with bamboo and grass hutments. It was amazing to see and learn what all could be done with bamboo. Meanwhile the vast primary covered jungle of the NEFA (North East Frontier Agency) loomed large and extended across the northern skyline.

A couple of days later, I was standing next to a jeep in the jungle in a sandy nala, looking for the bamboo cutters sent out by us, when without the slightest warning a large tusker elephant emerged from the jungle barely 75 yards distance from where we were and crossed the sandy nala in full view of us. He did not look either left or right. I was later to learn that elephants have very poor eye sight. The direction of the prevailing wind, must have been favourable for us, as the tusker paid no attention to us as he ambled past and entered the thick jungle on the far side of the sandy bed of the nala.

The fairly moist jungle was full of leeches and festooned with creepers. The few tribals we saw were Appatanis. The Inner Line forbade its crossing unless on official work. Roads, if any, were only just beginning to be constructed.

The two brigades of 4 Infantry Division (5 and 7 Brigades) were to be scattered over the vast area in "penny packets". Initially it was all very vague and uncertain. Later, 7 Infantry Brigade was earmarked for the Kameng Division, which had Tawang, Sela, Tenga and Bomdila. A one-tonner road was being constructed over the Eagles Nest ridge towards Tenga that would take a long time to get to Tawang. The Dalai Lama and his entourage had used this route while fleeing Tibet.

We were blissfully unaware of what was happening. Our battalion was to now be a part of 5 Infantry Brigade. Initially we were told that we were earmarked for going into Siang Division. We even did a reconnaissance trip to Along, which had a concrete World War II airfield. We were flown in a Dakota aircraft, overflying the Zero valley, which passed under us looking like a giant crater of an extinct volcano. On this trip, from Along, I accompanied Major Avasthy to Yekshing on the confluence of the Siyom and Siang Rivers.

At Yekshing, there was a 800-foot long cane bridge across the Siyom River. It consisted of cane tied up in a series of rings or circular loops which were held together by a steel wire rope. It was an amazing piece of engineering. It looked like a long tube through which a man could walk upright by supporting himself by holding on to the succession of cane rings. It swayed with

the wind, but otherwise was quite safe. Thick cane of about one inch diameter had been gathered from the jungle to make this ingenuous contraption.

Further downstream of the cane bridge, the Siyom drained into the Siang. The Siang originates in Tibet as the Tsang Po and flows into the plains of Assam. Just after flowing into Assam, it is joined by the Lohit, also coming from further east in Tibet, to become the mighty Bhramaputra. The water content of snow fed Siang and Lohit Rivers is enormous. During the monsoons the additional rain water leads to very destructive floods in the plains of Assam.

The two eastern Frontier Divisions of NEFA, Siang and Lohit, are named after the big rivers that flow through them. The Siang flowed into our area at Tuting, which was well upstream of Yekshing.

Militarily it seemed too vast an area to cover with the scant force that was being inducted. Somewhat later we learnt that there was a change and our battalion was now to be inducted into the extreme eastern Lohit Frontier Division. We learnt that we were to be entirely air lifted to Walong in the Lohit Frontier Division, which had an Assam Rifles platoon-size post there. Walong had a grass airstrip that could take Otter single engine transport aircraft.

Air maintenance of the Assam Rifles posts in the Lohit Valley was being carried out hitherto fore by Dakota aircraft operated by Kalinga Airways, on a contract basis. On our induction, the Air Force would undertake our air maintenance task using their fleet of Dakota aircraft operating from Jorhat Airbase. Thus, Jorhat Airbase was to be the focal point for our induction into Walong, using the single engine Otter Dehaviland light transport aircraft for troop lifting and supported by Dakota twin engine aircraft. Dakotas were the sturdy aircraft that had been the main workhorse of the Allied operations in Burma during the Second World War against the Japanese.

For the fairly long flight to Walong, an intermediate grass strip on the Digaru River was to be used, being called the Teju Airfield. A Company of our battalion was to be located here as a distant backup to the main buildup of the unit at Walong. After Teju the aircraft entered the narrow valley of the Lohit. It was a ten days march by foot from Walong to Teju. I was to undertake this long reconnaissance trek later in the year. The Assam Rifles had a well set up battalion headquarters some miles away at Lohitpur. Further away was Teju, the Frontier District Headquarters where the Political Officer or District Deputy Commissioner was based. All these were widely scattered with very thick primary forest in between. Large herds of wild elephants and wild buffalos roamed this thick jungle.

I am going ahead in giving you these facts as all this got set up by and by. In this narration of events we were yet to start the process of the induction in early 1960.

I was relieved of the QM's job to rejoin the Gujjar B Company, which was earmarked for being airlifted from Jorhat for induction into the Lohit valley at Walong. The company had moved by the circuitous route and collected at the Jorhat Airfield for induction. Move from the north bank of the Bhramaputra to the south bank was very time consuming in those days.

LOHIT FRONTIER DIVISION

As mentioned, the Battalion was to be inducted into the extreme eastern frontier division, the Lohit Frontier Division. This meant that we were to be flown upstream of the Lohit River and landed at Walong, at the grass landing strip on the right bank of the river. Preparatory to the induction by air into Walong, I joined the company at Jorhat Air Field. I was accommodated in a tent but was attached to the Air Force Officers Station Mess for my meals. It was a heaven sent opportunity to get to know the young group of Otter pilots that were to be flying us in to Walong eventually. It proved quite easy to make friends with the flyers as many of them were ex-NDA fellow cadets of the Academy days. This rapport was a great asset in the long run. This bonding of having been together in the Joint Services Wing days led to friendships of the lasting kind.

On the very first day I noticed a strange sight in the hat rack of the Air Force Mess when I hung up my beret with its Rajput hackle amongst the large number of Air Force grey side caps. An unusual sight was to see a blue sardar's pugree also hung up. I learnt later that the pugree belonged to Flying Officer Sandhu. He was completely bald. but otherwise sported a clipped sardars' beard. How he got into the habit of taking off his sardars pugree must remain a mystery, but it was very visible to me that Sandhu was a very popular flyer amongst the younger lot of pilots. Later I learnt that he had earlier been flying Dakotas, which he once flew dangerously low over a tea plantation airstrip, "strafing" some cattle grazing on it. I believe the matter got reported when some pieces of telephone wire were picked off the wing of his aircraft by the maintenance staff. Sandhu was 'ticked off' for the low flying during which he had gotten low enough to pick up some bits of telephone wire. However, he was now a popular member of the Otter Squadron. The Air Force lot seemed to like their 'daredevils'. I was to have an interesting event with him on my very first attempt to take a first look at Walong.

I sought and got permission to fly in one of the routine Assam Rifles Otter sorties to take a quick look around at Walong, prior to the beginning of our own induction. I got to the boarding area where the Assam Rifles Otter sortie was being loaded. I had no difficulty getting myself manifested on telling the pilot of my wanting to accompany him on the flight to Walong and back to take a first look at that place as we were to be inducted there soon. The pilot was none other than Flying Officer Sandhu, He asked me to hop in and asked me to occupy the co-pilots' seat next to his in the cockpit.

This was the only second or third time I was flying in an Otter, but this was the very first time in the co-pilot's seat. I gleefully got to the seat and strapped myself in with the safety harness and belts. I got a few minutes to glance at the control panels and instruments in front of the pilot's seat. This included the central panel between our seats having the three levers that controlled the propeller functions and the throttle. The Otter's instrument panel seemed simple enough. My curiosity satisfied, I sat back waiting for the pilot. The control column (also called Joy Stick) with which the pilot controlled the flight was in front of the pilot's seat, with the rudder pedals on the floor below. The Otter brakes were meant for the two front fixed under-carriage wheels. The rear wheel had to be locked in a fixed position after the pilot maneuvered the aircraft on the ground with the use of the brakes – with the single

engine providing the forward thrust. All this was interesting stuff and I watched as the pilot got into the seat and carried out all the preliminary checks before starting up the engine.

Sandhu had his earphones and mike around his neck through which he seemed to be speaking to the control tower. On starting up, over the noise of the engine I could only see things without hearing what was happening. All went well till we got to the runway centre line, prior to take off. Just after locking the rear wheel , the engine power was turned on full while the pilot sat on the brakes until the straining aircraft shot forward for the take off. All seemed to be going well, when a sudden gust of wind seemed to hit the tail of the aircraft in such a manner that it veered off the centre line. The drift was perceptible enough for the pilot to attempt straightening it out by using the rudder pedals.

I saw Sandhu lean forward and unlock the rear wheel to undertake the corrective action with the rudder pedals. Suddenly the aircraft seemed to further lurch off the centre line. At full throttle the aircraft was already straining to take off, and now it was gathering speed but hurtling away almost at right angle away from the runway. I could see the pilot struggling with the control column, using his left hand. His right hand had pushed the throttle and propeller controls to maximum. As the pilot struggled to control the aircraft, which had by now left the concrete runway, having got onto the rough grass on the side, gathering speed. Straight in front and in our way, was a red colored Bell helicopter, with its rotors moving slowly . The startled faces of the helicopter pilots, looking up at us as we flashed passed and over them. How we managed to avoid crashing into the helicopter remains a mystery. The Otter at full throttle was probably already straining to begin to lift a bit to get airborne.

Our troubles were far from over as we next flew across the wide drain, running parallel to the runway and now suddenly seemed headed straight for a Dakota aircraft being loaded and prepared

for an air drop. Flying Officer Sandhu was in a cold sweat by now and he desperately pulled the control column as far back as he could. Mercifully the roaring engine of the aircraft lifted the small Otter clear into the air to miss hitting the Dakotas by inches. The startled faces of the air maintenance men flashed past. We just barely missed hitting the wireless antenna wire of the Dakota, which connects the cockpit and the tail. It couldn't have been more than a couple of inches to spare. Suddenly we were flying and in the clear. I glanced back at the Assam rifles men in the back and saw their poker-faced expressions. They seemed blissfully unaware of what we had just been through.

The unusual take off of Sandhu's Otter had been seen by the control tower staff. It was suspected that he may have blown a tire during the take off. We were made to fly around for the fuel to get used up and also the tires were carefully examined with the help of binoculars from the ground. I could see Sandhu speaking on the intercom while all this was going on. Fire tenders were lined up as we were told to land. It went off smoothly and I sat in the co-pilot's seat as the Group Captain Station Commander gave Sandhu an apparent talking to and probably a dressing down.

The Station Commander, a handsome silver-haired officer, asked me if I still wanted to fly to Walong with Sandhu. I did not know what to say. All I knew was that we had a close call.

This event allowed me to get to friendly terms with most of the younger flyers of the Otter Squadron. Dali Gandhi, Bhake Lal, Hundal and a host of others, and of course Sandhu, became friends of an enduring kind. They would bring letters from home and bring cheer to us at Walong, whenever they would come to visit us. Dali Gandhi once even flew on a holiday to bring us a Chistmas cake from Firpos of Calcutta.

WALONG

Walong was almost an hour and a half in flying time from Jorhat. About half the distance was over the sprawling Bhramputra River, before the aircraft overflew the vast forest covered Teju area and entered the narrow Lohit Valley. The River had cut a deep canyon-like passage through the jungle covered mountains. Very sparsely populated, it gave you an eerie feeling flying upstream along the meandering river. The cliff-like heights on both sides had a forbidding look about them.

At Walong the valley opened up, with a complete change in type of vegetation. The altitude of the grass strip was about 5500 feet above sea level. Both sides of the river was covered by extensive Chil Pine *Pinus Longifolia forest*. The river here had a slight bend in it where a small Lama village, called Walong was tucked into a side. On the far bank there was another small Lama village named Dong. Both villages were small and untidy, and both males and females wearing predominantly black clothing. Small patches of paddy cultivation were tucked into the hillsides at places.

Conspicuously the Miju Mishmi Tribals had their villages down stream of Walong. The Miju Mishmis would freely visit Walong as it was the Frontier civil administration base, where Mr.Ao a very cheerful Naga Officer, was located.

Beside the grass airstrip the Civil Administrations representatives little office was set up. Mr. Ao, being the Officer in

Charge of the Frontier Station, had his family residing with him. Mrs. Ao would have a baby strapped on her back, and a brood of kids following her.

Walong being a Frontier Station, was emphasized by a full-size national flag fluttering in the strong windy conditions. The strong prevailing wind down the valley would abruptly change at about midday and thereafter would blow strongly in the opposite direction of flow of the river. The flag and the windsock would daily be visible undergoing this phenomenon. It was dangerous for the Otter aircraft operating there as it was not safe to land if the wind direction had changed

On my first visit to Walong, I was struck with the natural beauty of the place. The national flag looked so impressive as it caught the full flow of the strong breeze.

I have gone ahead with this narration as all the buildup in Walong was a painfully slow process. It took many months to get going. By the end of 1960 we had managed to get most of the battalion and a Heavy Mortar Battery's elements inducted. The routine of leave and Army courses kept us coming and going. Movement in and out of Walong was severely restricted due to the limitation of airlift.

By early 1962, having been in NEFA for almost three years, a Kumoan Battalion started to replace us at Walong. We were to be collected back next to the railhead for our de-induction. We were to move back to where we had started from. All move was slow and time consuming.

*****

Walong – Chhu Pass 1961

In July 62, when the battalion had assembled for a move to Mathura, their next peace station, I got posted to the Indian Military Academy at Dehradun as a Platoon Commander. Lt Col MS Rikh may have had a hand in my getting this 'home' posting. He knew that Usha was expecting our second child by October.

Barely a month after leaving the battalion, and my joining at Dehradun, events owing to the sudden developments in the Kameng district the battalion got drawn into the disastrous war against the Chinese as a part of 7 Brigade on the Nam Ka Chu. The battalion suffered 283 All Ranks killed on 20 th October 1962 morning. Colonel Rikh and about 160 All ranks were taken prisoners by the Chinese. Bulk of the captured were wounded in the Battle. The battalion had ceased to exist as a fighting unit.

There is a poignant personal irony for me, in having escaped the fate of my comrades in that bitter struggle of October 1962.

You cannot choose your battlefield,
God does that for you
But you can plant a standard
Where a standard never flew

Nathaniel Crane 'The Colours'

* * * * *

THE LIMHAIPUR TIGERS

I would like to draw the reader back in time to early 1960, As the induction into the Lohit Frontier Division would take a long time, the annual leave found me getting home in early January. My parents had been on a long spell of leave in Europe in 1958-59, where my mother was undergoing treatment for a very severely debilitating form of arthritis at a place called Badgastian in Switzerland. Father was posted to Bilaspur on his return. Earlier in 1946 Father had a short spell of a posting as the district second-in-command. He was now the district head, waiting to get promoted as Commissioner. Usha was waiting there for my homecoming.

Father had bought me a Winchester . 375 Magnum bolt action Model 70 rifle. This weapon was considered the best all-round weapon for big game shikar. It used the improved Nitro ammunition, firing a 300-grain or alternately a 270-grain bullet. It was the latest state-of-the art caliber shikar weapon, having a modified Rimless Rimmed cartridge. The rifle had a wide 'V' back sight that helped in quickly aligning the weapon. It had a very handy canvas cover as a carrying case.

The Sal jungles around Kanha, extend further eastwards to the Bilaspur District. The jungles around Amarkantak, from where the Narbada, Sone and the Mahanadi rivers originate and flow outwards respectively towards the west, north-east, and south-east; were considered some of the finest Shikar districts. Names like *Kabir-Chabutra*, *Lamni*, and *Achanakmar* were well-known shooting blocks. These were extensively interconnected with Sal and bamboo jungle, seemingly endlessly.

One prominent 'tongue' like projection of this mass of jungle was towards the south, towards Pandaria (a Tehsil Town) in the Bilaspur District. Several small villages and hamlets on the periphery of this 'tongue' of forest would repeatedly lose cattle to tigers operating from this projection of the forest. Pandaria was connected by a good road with the District Town of Bilaspur. A kill taking place in any of the villages next to the 'tongue' of forest could be reported by midday at Bilaspur.

Limhaipur, was one such hamlet of about ten untidy looking huts. The frequent loss of cattle to tigers was a severe blow to the impoverished owners. Cattle generally looked very poor and undernourished.

On the first occasion we got word of a kill having taken place near Limhaipur by afternoon at Bilaspur, but the distance to be covered only allowed us to get to the site of the kill after darkness had already set in. When we took a chance and got to the prepared machan, the tiger had removed the kill, leaving a knawed leg behind. Nothing came of from the impromptu beat that we had next morning. We drove back in the Jeep next morning after leaving more specific instructions in the event of a fresh kill. Tying up a suitable machan was also a part of the future plan. Timely arrival was critical for the plan.

It was a rainy day when we got word of the next kill at Limhaipur. It was the village pot-makers pony that had been taken this time. Both tigers and leopards are very fond of horse flesh. In an earlier story I have recounted how the man-eating leopard of Jhilpa had met his end when he had made a kill in an orange grove of a village donkey. The Jhilpa man-eater had turned up at the kill, breaking his usual habit of not returning to a kill.

When we got to Limhaipur this time there was about an hour's

daylight left. We left the Jeep outside the village and got to the already set up machan, which was about a fifteen minutes walk from where we had been met on the track leading to the village. To protect me in the winter drizzle, apart from wearing a warm trench coat, I was using my broad, brimmed Gorkha hat. I settled down in the comfortable machan, properly wrapped up to protect me from the constant drizzle, the wide brim of my Gorkha hat shielding my face. The .375 Magnum Rifle with a three-cell torch attached, was so kept that I could use it when required with minimum fuss. Owing to the rain, however I had covered the weapon with the blanket, with me to the extent possible. I felt I would have plenty of time once the tiger started eating the kill.

The kill had been really gorged upon as very little flesh seemed left. As a precaution, Father suggested that the kill be tied down to a peg. This was done, using one of the ribs, which was fastened to the peg. This was necessary to avoid the skeletal remains not being removed without my doing something about it. The rain made the place soaking wet.

The rain made the sit up a different experience. The sound of pitter-patter of rain drops on the leaves around me deadened all other telltale sound. Consequently, I did not hear the tiger approach the kill, and pick it up and move off before I could react. The tie-down with the peg had not helped as the rib just seemed to slip out. It took me a little time to realize that I'd been left "high and dry" by the tiger. When I switched on the torch light the blank space where the kill had been was empty. The disturbance in the wet short grass indicated the direction the kill had been taken by the tiger. I felt really foolish, not knowing what to do next.

The rifle had a sling, and removing the torch to get going, I collected the second weapon a shotgun and other stuff and climbed down from the machan. I managed to get back to where we had started from near a *peepal* tree. The village was some distance away. I walked into Deva-pitta's presence, feeling acutely embarrassed and disappointed. I soon joined Father on the string *charpai* and warmed my hands on the small fire which filled the hut with more smoke than warmth.

After hearing me out the villagers seemed to console me by saying that there was more than one tiger in the area and that a beat on the morrow would bring them out. At that time I felt they were saying all this to let me overcome the disappointment of the evening.

The next morning was a clear and sunny day. The jungle looked fresh and sparkling with the overnight rain having abated after midnight. The villagers gathered to carry out the beat. Hopes of success got boosted with the elders saying that it was a certainty that the tigers would come out in the beat. They all kept saying that In the past this particular beat had always yielded results.

There was already a sturdy machan constructed some time earlier, on which I was to overlook and cover one of the likely route to be possibly taken by the tiger. The expected escape route lay along a shallow, dry nala bed. The nala was itself formed by two shallow water courses, the junction of the two being overlooked by me from the machan. The beat covered the major portion of the mile wide 'tongue' of jungle, starting from where I had sat up the previous night.

In other words, the major portion of the jungle from which the cattle lifting tigers would sally out and take a toll of the cattle from the scattered villages from all around the broad strip was being beaten. As mentioned earlier, Limhaipur suffered greatly by this depredation.

A second machan covered the next likely route of escape for the tigers, also along a shallow nala. Deva-pitta occupied this second machan. He was armed with his trusted old .405 Winchester rifle. Of the two, my machan was considered the more favoured one.

After the beat had been in progress some twenty-five minutes or so, I saw a tiger walking briskly along the far bank of the nala I was

overlooking towards my left. As it sprang across the further dry water course my shot at its heart region, made him stagger in his stride, but he managed to keep going, using the further watercourses shelter.

In the meanwhile, following almost the same route a second tiger briskly broke cover to jump across the nala junction. My shot knocked him down, but he managed to get up and snarling with pain made a dash to get further. He flinched again at my second shot but staggered further away into some cover. I had hardly time to reflect on the situation of having both the tigers in the same *general* area of cover. Having two wounded tigers in the same area could pose a serious problem later.

The beat was far from over and from the noise and din they were making, it seemed there was more to come. I tore open a fresh packet of ammunition to reload the . 375 Magnum rifle, when a movement in my front drew me looking down at a third tiger as he rapidly moved towards my tree. He would have passed right under my machan, had my shot not turned him away towards the left. He galloped away obliquely to the approaching line of beaters. I held my breath with the fear of him catching a beater off guard as he blundered backwards. Mercifully, nothing happened as the tiger had collapsed before causing any harm.

The three were retrieved as they had not gone any great distance. Two were young males with beautiful winter coats. The third was a sub-adult tigress.

*****

I can sense how the reader will react on reading the above account of the Limhaipur tigers. I was then just 24 years old, and only learnt much later in life that tigers stayed many years with the mother till they take off independently to fend for themselves. Years before at Adilabad we had chanced upon a family of five together – obviously a mother with fully grown cubs. Much later

one learnt that even the male and father shares a close relationship with the family sometimes. Much very valuable research on the tiger has been undertaken in India since Independence

Since there seemed to be an abundance of tigers country wide, the knowledge of tiger's family life was not realized. Even Jim Corbett's writings do not touch upon this aspect. During Project 'Tiger' the scientific research largely based on Project 'Tiger' protected areas allowed such research. Dedicated work done by the young scientists and scholars contributed significantly under the Wild Life Institute of India.

What has very significantly helped is the great technology in the use of the camera. Telephoto lens and video filming has contributed significantly to the knowledge of wildlife. During the British Raj a few photograph oriented people tried taking photographs and making films, like F W Champion and Jim Corbett himself. But all this has changed for the better and the 'Tiger' has received due attention. Unlike Africa, Indian jungle needed sophisticated equipment to reveal its mystery.

The debate goes on to somehow protect the dwindling number of tigers in India. Sanctuaries and protected reserves have become jungle zoos to attract the tourist. Tigers have adapted to this exposure to humans and it is difficult to relate to the tiger of yore when one sees the animal ignoring crowds of tourist spilling out of gypsy jeeps, wielding cameras . Tigers in these sanctuaries also ignore the presence of elephants which play an important role in first locating the animal and then helping the camera wielding tourist to get a close in look for photography. It serves a purpose and can be accepted as it is.

The tiger has suffered enormously in other areas. It has steadily lost out in the man-animal conflict owing to the uncontrolled and wanton destruction of even minimal forest cover which enabled the animal to survive. Tiger population countrywide largely depended upon cattle-lifting. Poor quality cattle provided the major share of what kept the predators fed. The tiger and leopard never could sustain on deer and such like prey by itself.

In Jim Corbett's narrations, most of the time it was cattle that were kills. In the Kumoan hills today one hardly ever hears of a tiger. Man has exterminated the tiger by fair or foul means .

Take the case of the recognized shooting areas of old time CP, later reorganized as Madhya Pradesh. Wholesale exploitation of 'Shikar' as a money earning device by ruthless politically powerful parties, made hay and decimated the tiger and leopard /panther under official patronage.

Complete banning of shikar has hardly helped. No check and balance is kept and any semblance of actual control of wildlife is given just lip service.

ELEPHANTS
(*ELEPHAS MAXIMUS- LINNAEUS*)

In the Lohit Frontier Division the company located at Teju airfield on the banks of the wide Digaru Nala, had dense jungle surrounding it. We were however left alone by the herds of elephants residing within the neighboring jungle, though sometimes one heard the trumpeting sounds and often saw the copious elephant droppings on the roads in the area.

Once , I accompanied Mr. Chowkamin Gohain, a prominent tribal leader and a nominated member of the Indian Rajya Sabha, on a pad elephant ride. We rode northwards on Mr. Gohain's pad elephant, going upstream of the airfield and along the sandy bed of the wide Digaru. The Digaru's wide sandy expanse enabled the sudden discharge of water in the catchment area upstream to quickly drain into the mainstream Lohit River in the south. Woe betide any one getting caught in the sudden surge of fast flowing water during the flash floods. The wide sandy bed was strewn with some rocks and boulders.

We had nothing specific in mind that morning. After proceeding some distance, our attention was drawn to the presence of some scavenger birds and a couple of jackals close to the decaying carcass of an elephant, somewhat buried in the sand. It was decomposing and approaching it was not a pleasant experience. A large hole was visible on one side, exposing the rotting innards. A jackal actually jumped out of the opening, all covered with gore on our approach.

We got down from our pad elephant and despite the smelly task, proceeded to examine the dead elephant and the surroundings. Most of the tell-tale marks were obliterated by the vultures and jackal activity. However, on carefully looking around we came to the conclusion that a pair of tigers may have killed the elephant which seemed to have been trapped in the sand. The evidence was in the presence of pug marks of a pair of tigers over a wide area, where the struggle had taken place. However, it was several days old tell-tale marks and we could be wrong in our surmise. Mr. Gohoin mentioned that after a heavy downpour of rain, some patches of the wet sand become dangerous for heavy animals who sink into the resultant quicksand. This may have immobilized the elephant and the tigers seemingly took advantage of the situation.

*****

The next opportunity to get a closer look at a herd of elephants was in the Corbett National Park. I was then posted at the Military Academy at Dehradun. During a midterm break in 1963 I had accompanied a party of Gentlemen Cadets on an angling expedition on the Ramganga River, which flows through a considerable length of the Corbett National Park. We were camping at the Gairal Rest House, upstream on the crystal clear watered Ramganga River. Lt Col Joe Pinto of the Signal Corps, was the senior accompanying officer. Joe was an outstanding sportsman, and a great enthusiast of Mahseer fishing. He was mainly responsible to draw me to the sport of angling. I was a slow starter at the sport and initially could not catch anything, whilst most of the party were doing well by catching some of the golden mahseer of varying sizes in the beautiful clear water of the Ramganga.

The Corbett Park nestles between the Himalayan foothills and the Shivalik hills. The Ramganga flows through from the east to west in the wide valley formed by the foothills in the north and enclosed by the Shivalik Ranges chain of jungle covered low hills

on the south. Most of the area of the Park has dense Sal forest in the eastern portion, but opens out into a vast grassy meadow on both sides of the river downstream. Dhikala is a small forest department establishment with a popular comfortable Rest House located somewhat in the middle. A dam was under construction downstream on the Ramganga as it cut its way across the Shivalik Range at Kalagarh. In 1963 this dam was under construction and has since been completed, resulting in the western portion of the vast meadow being flooded to form a large lake.

At Gairal, somewhat disappointed with my inability to catch fish, I sought the company of Captain Arvind Inamdar, a fellow instructor at the Academy and who had come with us on the trip, for an afternoon of wildlife viewing in the area near Dhikala. Beyond Dhikala the forest road ran in a straight line along the edge of the thick forest on one side and the vast open grassy meadow on the other. A sturdy machan on some tall trees within the edge of the jungle placed you at a vantage point for viewing deer and other animals that came out in the evening to the salt lick located in the open grass maidan.

Arvind was from the Sikh Regiment battalion that had been grieviosly roughed up by the Chinese in the area adjacent to Tawang and later at Sela in the Kameng District of NEFA (now Arunachal) during October and November 1962. During the Kashmir operations in October 1947, his Sikh unit had blunted the raiders thrust near Baramula but lost their Commanding Officer in the process.

We, that is Captain Arvind Inamdar and I, got the Colonel's permission to borrow his jeep to take us to the Dhikala area to spend the afternoon and evening in one of the wildlife viewing machans overlooking the salt-lick. On a previous casual passing visit the salt-lick was teeming with Chital and hog deer in the late afternoon. The Forest Department sturdy machan was placed high enough for viewing even elephants. Ali, the driver of the jeep dropped us at the selected machan and took the jeep away to the Dhikala Rest House area. We instructed Ali to come and collect us as night set in. On second thought, I had asked Ali to keep an eye on our area during the daylight hours, should we require him earlier. We would wave a white handkerchief to attract his attention if we wanted him to come back earlier for us.

We had climbed into the machan well before the expected time for the wildlife to appear. Sadly nothing seemed to be happening and we were perplexed that no chital (*Axis axis*) or hog deer (*Axis porcinus*) seemed to be interested in the salt-lick this evening. We did hear a loud abrupt sound once, but could make nothing of it at the time. Realising that something was different this evening, I asked Arvind as to what we should do. He agreed that it seemed futile to keep sitting over the salt- lick with nothing to view. We accordingly climbed down and started walking back on the forest road to Dhikala. Ali, the driver saw us and started up the jeep to come to us.

In the meanwhile as we proceeded back along the road, we saw a cow elephant with a calf in an opening in the jungle. It dawned

Sambar stag sprouting fresh antlers

on me that a herd of elephants were waiting to emerge onto the salt- lick area as the evening closed in. This explained the absence of the other animals not appearing. It seemed prudent to get away from the edge of the jungle to avoid accidently blundering into the elephants as they seemed to be waiting to come out onto the open grassland in which the salt- lick was located.

Jeep driver Ali got to us soon and as we started to drive away, it occurred to me that we had made a mistake coming down from the vantage viewpoint of the machan as it would have given us an unique chance of a close look in at the herd of elephants around the salt-lick. Taking matters in hand quickly, I asked Ali to turn the jeep around, and again and boldly drive at a steady pace along the forest road, back to the machan we had abandoned earlier. Driver Ali held his nerve as at least three elephants had crossed the road by now and were uncomfortably close as we drove past. We managed to get to the machan and leaving the jeep on the road climbed up into the safety of the machan. We were all a little

breathless as we climbed up. Ali, the driver looking down at his jeep parked on the road beneath us.

As dusk set in we could now see as many as about forty adult and sub-adult elephants scattered in a wide circular manner. Some mother animals with young calves were kept in the inner protected area. As the evening turned to night a bright moon lit up the area for us to get a better idea how things were shaping. It was fascinating watching the pattern of the herd's spread. The bright moonlight was a great help for our viewing.

A young sub-adult tusker ambled along the forest road until it almost blundered into Ali's jeep. He let off a startled trumpeting scream on smelling the presence of us humans and the petrol fumes coming from the jeep's engine. The young tusker stood back in a defiant uncertain stance, while his earlier scream had invited a large tusker to hasten to his aid. The massive hulk of this large tusker, was really awe inspiring. We could see his huge tusks gleaming in the bright moonlight from pretty close from the safety of the sturdy machan. This tusker approached the jeep, and stood stock still in a menacing manner to react to any hostile movement from the jeep.

After a few minutes the tension eased off and the flapping of his ears resumed. Slowly the big tusker moved away and ambled off towards the herd. Arvind and I realized that we had a close exposure of a rare kind. Usually the dominant male remains outside the main herd, following it at a distance. How quickly this massive and powerful animal had responded to the alarm squeal of the sub-adult on seeing the jeep, remains a mystery. He seemed to have appeared suddenly from nowhere.

What we would have had to say if the jeep had been roughed up by the elephant in the Courts of Inquiry that would have followed, became a part of the evening banter.

We all climbed down quickly when we got the opportunity and Ali brought us safely back from a most memorable evening with a large herd of elephants in the Corbett Wildlife Park.

Later, in the summer of 1964 while still posted at the Military Academy, my brother Vijay was posted in the Dehradun Sub-Area on the staff. He got a permit for the shooting of three elephants in the Barkot Shooting Block in the vicinity of Rishikesh. We were told that the herd of about fifty animals had crossed over the Ganga River and were causing considerable damage in the area and were thus earmarked for destruction. The herd usually re-crossed the Ganga into the abundant jungle on the eastern bank. However, this year they were showing no sign of going back. The forest department in their wisdom had proscribed the herd for destruction.

We later learnt that there were several shikar parties issued such permits. We had a pretty close call and a near accident because of this thoughtless step of the forest department staff.

We carefully prepared for the task in hand. An elephant's skull kept in the Forest Research Institute museum gave us some insight as to how to go about it. The big dome like forehead of the elephant is largely a honeycomb of bony mass and protects the brain of the animal from the front. A frontal shot has to be taken to get to the brain through the nasal passage leading into the trunk. A frontal fatal shot to the brain has to be angled upwards to be affective. Which means the shikari has to be very close to the elephant. Alternately, a better option is to hit in the centre of a saucer shaped depression from the side. The prominent saucer like depression is located midway between the ear opening and the eyes. Both of us brothers being quite inexperienced, were uncertain and nervous about this endeavour.

I got hold of the survey maps of the area of the Barkot Shooting Block to study the lie of the land to try and anticipate where we might encounter the herd. The forest firelanes and roads have a role to play. The maps enabled us to quickly grasp the lie of the land and drainage pattern of the nalas of the area.

We camped at the Barkot Forest Rest house, with Usha and Vijay's

wife Indu, handling the logistics. My black Ambassador car was to provide us some mobility. Old friend and shikari-cum-guide Nathu had also joined us in the venture. Beside my .375 Magnum Winchester Model 70 rifle, we had the Academy .450/400 double barrel Rifle. We were very short of solid bullets for both the weapons as these were just not available. Captain Sushil Pillai of the Assam Regiment, had an excellent .450 Jeffreys double barreled weapon. His was a very powerful weapon for the task. Sushil's Father had been the Chief Conservator of Forest in the old time CP and later Madhya Pradesh. Being colleagues at the Academy, Sushil also bonded well with us because of our 'Jungly' background. Sushil was to be with us on our final encounter with the herd. His powerful rifle was to be a useful addition to our firepower.

Our map study proved helpful as we had two major encounters with the herd of elephants in an area we had somewhat predicted and anticipated from our study of the map. On the first occasion we were accompanied by Nathu Shikari and were that morning, following the clear trail of the herd. Elephant feet knock down the tufts of rough grass in a manner that leaves no doubt which way the animal was going. We were trailing the herd easily, as nearly forty animals had moved that way in a broad swath. We had paused at one place briefly when we caught two little Jungli murghi chicks, attempting to conceal themselves in the dry Sal leaves that littered the jungle floor.

Just then we heard the sound of rifle shots, fired in quick succession in the direction of where the herd ahead of us had gone. I realized immediately that we were in grave danger of being trampled when the herd tried going back the way they had passed earlier. Sure enough, we could soon hear the rising surge of sound like an approaching storm of the animals as they moved through the dry Sal windfalls on the ground, in some haste. The surging sound grew rapidly, coming closer every moment. Suddenly the herd almost burst upon us as we were clearly in the way. Realising that the herd was wheeling towards us in their haste to get away, in some desperation I fired at the medium sized female on the inner flank, to divert the herd from coming onto us. The effort succeeded and the lot just thundered past us, barely missing us.

Some other Shikaris had come upon the herd ahead of us and had nearly had us trampled by the panicking herd by shooting at the elephants. We later learnt that it was an American missionary named Taylor who had brought down a female elephant in the melee. It was unknown to us that other shikaris had been also permitted to operate in the same area as us.

We had barely avoided a mishap, and were just beginning to breathe easy, when I chanced to look up while picking up the spent cartridge cases of the two rounds fired by me. As I bent down to pick up the two empties, I had fortunately kept my eyes scanning the jungle adjacent to where the herd had emerged to go past us. Some slight flicker of a movement which my eye had caught led to my realizing that there was an elephant standing very still in the light and shade of the Sal trees. On looking carefully, I soon detected that what had caught my eye was the tuft of hair at the end of the elephant's tail which the elephant had flipped . It was amazing that such a large animal blended completely in the light and shade of the jungle. It was very lucky that I had detected the animals presence. It was the dominant male of the herd who was standing stock still to take stock of the situation. He was all set to follow the main herd and we were squarely in his way.

I quickly drew Vijay's attention to this threat and asked him to get next to a Sal tree on my left flank. We were just in time as the tusker seemingly unaware of us strode forward towards us. He seemed to be in no haste and came steadily on towards where I was. I had meanwhile placed myself behind the bole of a thick Sal tree to better rest the rifle against .

The tusker looked uniformly grey in color and his head nodded rhythmically, up and down as he kept steadily coming on towards me. His ears flapping as he moved unhurriedly. I waited for him

to get closer to get a frontal shot on that bump on his trunk. He was not as big or massive as the tusker I had seen in Corbett Park the previous year, but was still a towering specimen advancing towards me. He seemed totally unaware of us.

The situation had developed so fast and unexpectedly that I did not get time to realize the grave danger we were in. As he got closer, I tried to remain steady and calm. He was almost towering over me and I must have lost my nerve, for my shot at the olfactory bulge on the trunk did not bring him down. The shot of the powerful rifle at this close range however, made him recoil back a few paces and turn desperately away. Vijay from a flank tried to get a shot at the side temple which knocked him down momentarily. But he almost swung back to get onto his feet and thundered away as Vijay tried to get another shot at him. Feeling utterly foolish, we were both holding empty rifles, as the injured animal made his getaway

Shaken and feeling uncertain we made our way back to the Barkot Forest Rest House. We had been very lucky that we had escaped injury that day. The midsummer heat in the Sal jungle had favoured us as elephants depend greatly on smell that the wind carries. The huge animal has poor eye sight but a formidable sense of smell.

Later that evening we met the Divisional Forest Officer and conveyed our feelings in no uncertain terms at allowing other parties of shikaris to be operating in the same area as us. We told him of our close call that afternoon. We also met Mr. Taylor, the American Missionary Shikari, who very generously gifted me some Silver Tipped Ammunition for my rifle as I was now left with only a few soft nosed bullets which were quite unsuitable for the task in hand. Lucky for me, that he was using a similar .375 magnum rifle like mine.

What however proved very helpful was Sushil Pillai joining us with his very powerful . 450 Jeffreys double barreled rifle for our next encounter.

THE SECOND ENCOUNTER

It took us a couple of days to recover our composure and self confidence after our first encounter with the elephants. We were having serious misgivings about our venture. We were beginning to realize that we had perhaps bitten off more than what we could chew. However, we had gone too far to extricate from the effort.

Sushil Pillai and Nathu Shikari were with us on that morning when we next ran into the same herd. It was in the vicinity of our earlier encounter. This time the entire herd seemed to panic at getting wind of us and trumpeting loudly began to try to get away from us. Reluctant to lose contact, we rashly gave chase. I sensed trouble as the knowledge of the ground had made me aware that the herd was being driven towards a open fire lane and forest road junction. I realized that the herd would begin to rebound back and would refuse to cross the open fire lane. As I expected the whole lot turned around and came at us to get away. We had spread out in the earlier chase and I found myself getting the full focus of attention from perhaps the largest female of the herd. She had her trunk raised and pointing at me from the time I saw her. The ground seemed to quake with the whole herd hurtling back.

She was the matriarchal leader and was easily the biggest animal in the herd. Quite unaware of where my companions were, I realized I had to deal with her on my own as she came thundering at me. As she bore down on me I tried the frontal shot option. It failed to bring her down, but the powerful rifle shot made her turn her head enough for me to quickly reload and get my next shot at the saucer like depression between her eye and ear opening. At this her legs seemed to collapse suddenly and she fell forward in a heap. I yelled to the others to get quickly in the lee of the fallen animal to escape being trampled by the herd in its mad rush to get away past us. We all just managed to scramble into the safety of the space next to the fallen elephant. It was a touch and go situation. With knees knocking with fright, we all realized that we had just got away from a tight situation.

We came out of the area to get over the tension and get our wits together. When we returned to where the fallen female lay we saw an amazing sight. The tusker stood leaning on her, still bleeding from the earlier wounds. There was also another female close by. We found the matriarch female I had brought down was still alive and breathing. The shot had paralysed her as she lay in a heap. Vijay had the unpleasant task of dispatching her and the tusker. It was a touching display of family bonding and we were quite shaken at this.

What made things worst was to find that there was a very young calf whose mother was amongst the females killed. The pathetic efforts of the little fellow to remain beside the fallen mother or rejoin the herd were heart rendering. Finally, the Forest department staff got hold of it and even gave the calf a feed of milk from a beer bottle – before they took it away.

To this day I feel the great remorse of having been instrumental in the event just narrated. The elephant is essentially such a gentle giant, with a great family sense of togetherness. In India it is worshipped as the loveable Ganesha. The heady thrill of blood sport and the reckless habit of daring do cannot be wished away as a compulsive enough urge to perform as reason enough for such indulgence.

THE NILGIRI BISON OR GAUR
(*BOS GAURUS*)

During a short break for midterm at the Staff College at Wellington, I got a shooting license from the Wildlife authorities of the area to try for a bison. Mr. Rajan, of the Cinconna Department, our neighbor in Upper Conoor, joined me in the effort.

The license specified that the sportsman must ensure that the trophy sought, in the form of a head of a bull Bison must have a minimum 33 inches span from one tip of the horn to the other measured along the outer curvature. Additionally it was laid down that each horn must be at least 18 inches circumference in girth at its base. It was left to the sportsman how he was to judge that the quarry had the minimum specified dimensions during the hunt. After the shoot, the head of the bison shot had to be produced before the Forest Department for inspection. This made the task a tricky one. I had no idea how these requirements would be met. The size of the animal's head would have to be judged by its appearance and would involve some guess work. Mr. Rajan and I discussed the matter and decided that we would employ a local guide cum *shikari* who should help us.

We drove past Ooty, taking the sharply descending road past the Mutanad Defile down to Seyur, close to Masnigudi. We stayed in a forest guard's hut, with Rajan helping in overcoming the language problem. Rajan was a Tamilian, fluent in Tamil but the Forest Guard and the guide we got spoke mainly Kannarese. So the interesting mix of us got going with a lot of unanswered questions.

The flat yellow grass covered plain has a park like scattering of stringy trees through which we had to approach the abruptly rising northern slopes of the Nilgiris. The Nilgiris rise sharply for several thousand feet, towering above, but the lower grass covered slopes are favoured ground by some herds of bison. The second day of our toiling up and down the area, we had just had a snack lunch and were resting our tired feet, when we sighted a small herd of bison on the distant slope behind us. We had failed to see them on our way up as we had been defiladed by the lie of the slope above us.

It was appreciated that keeping the wind factor in mind, it was best to approach the browsing herd from below. The bisons were grazing and moving slowly upslope. A direct approach from a flank was ruled out as we would have been detected by the animals well before we could get close enough to them.

We detoured from downhill and then began a slow and steady climb upslope in the wake of the herd. They had grazed through the area as was evident from fresh dung that we saw at places. As we gained height, we knew they were somewhere above us feeding in the tall grass. We cautiously moved through the scattered trees on the slopes, trying to stalk the herd. The downward wind direction in the afternoon from the towering nilgiris above us also helped.

There was a grass covered rocky flat topped ledge that shielded us from being seen by the bisons who were feeding upslope in a scattered manner. I climbed silently onto the rocky flat top from its side and the others soon joined me. The four of us were thus facing uphill, with a sharp drop behind us owing to the configuration of the rock shelf we had climbed onto. We were too engrossed in looking uphill where a visible bison was rubbing his forehead against a sapling. The bison was about fifty yards uphill initially and his head rubbing against the sapling was bending and shaking the tree violently. We watched silently and could now see more of him to realize that he was fine looking bull bison. I tried in whispered conversation to ask the guide if the head was of the permissible dimension. Meanwhile as we were watching the bison unaware of us, turned slowly downhill and started moving casually downslope towards us. Being unsure of the suitability of the bull as a trophy I withheld taking a shot at the animal as he just kept moving towards us.

A Gaur (Bison in Kanha) 1995

As I raised the rifle to cover the animals throat for a frontal shot, I realized that he was ambling and stumbling along towards us but was still quite unaware of us. He was soon getting much too close for comfort and I realized that we were in a predicament as we could not step backward as we were. The guide with us

realising the sudden danger of the massive bison bull almost stumbling onto us made a deliberate throaty sound. The bison was now just about fifteen paces away and he abruptly jerked to a sudden halt when he saw us, his eyes suddenly flashed defiantly. Fortunately the four of us stood rock still. I had already lowered the rifle as he was too close now, and I realised that I could not but provoke him by any hasty action. The weapon however was still roughly pointing towards the animal.

As we stood frozen with fear at this sudden confrontation, I saw the look in his eyes slowly undergoing a change as he sized us up. With a snort and defiant shake of his massive head he slowly turned to a flank and then unhurriedly moved away. He had us completely at his mercy, but chose to let things pass. We quietly moved away without even speaking to each other for several minutes. We got off the rocky ledge the way we had climbed it from a flank.

It had struck me then as we trudged back that no trophy could match the memory of the grand and magnificent animal as he kept looking down at us. His horns seem to glow amber and grey. His nose had some grass sticking to it and I could clearly see the 'naughty boy' leather pattern on it. His eyes were quite different from the fixed glass eyes of the bison trophies in the Staff College Officers' Mess.

We made our way back after the incredible experience that we had that afternoon. As I led the way back, a grey jungle fowl startled me as it rose up suddenly from the grass.

As the evening faded into dusk a tiger called once from somewhere in the distance behind us.

It was perhaps a case of 'sour grapes' at going home after an unsuccessful trip. But it surely was a deeply felt moment of it being a turning point in this game of big game shooting.

JUST PLAIN SOLDIERING

On termination of the Staff College course, I was assigned to a new raising of the Rajput Regiment, which I joined at Fatehgarh after a months leave at Dehradun. My parents had settled there after Deva-Pitta retired from government service in 1961. They acquired a house on Turner Road leading into Clement Town. Having spent two full years at the Joint Services Wing then located at Clement Town, it was a pleasant thought that our family home would be in those surroundings.

Meanwhile after a few months 18 Rajput, my new battalion was moved to Misamari in the east, where many years before, we had arrived from the Shimla Hills with the 2nd Battalion in December 1959. It was now 1965 and the new unit I was with now had to train hard to form a well knit outfit. After the disastrous 1962 War with China, we had a purposeful task to get things going. 18 Rajput had a very erudite and serious first Commanding Officer in Lt Col Zail Singh. An outstanding athlete in his younger days, he had served earlier in more then one Rajput unit till he got the task of raising our new unit. He was very fond of the study of history in general and military history in particular. We soon had a good collection of books in the new units officers' mess library.

* * * * *

During the 1965 War with Pakistan 18 Rajput was rushed by train to the west, but missed out on any major commitment. Near

Ludhiana we had a Pak B-57 bomber drop a few bombs on us in the concentration area. A night later I was returning after having the recoil-less antitank guns bore-sight tested at the Naraingarh field firing ranges, we passed through Ambala early in the morning. The Pakistani Air Force had bombed the Ambala Air Field during the previous night. A large bomb had also struck the church and destroyed its tower. I managed to take a hurried look. In the still smouldering rubble of the church tower, hundreds of blue rock pigeons lay dead in contorted pathetic shapes.

However, by 22 September a cease fire had been declared and we were shifted to the Sirhind Canal bund to await further developments.

Shortly after the ceasefire took place, I took some leave and managed my way by hitch-hiking to where my brother Vijay's battalion (20 Rajput) were holding the Alhar railway station (as part of 14 Division) in the Sailkot Sector, on the loop line connecting Sialkot and Chawinda. The fresh telltale traces of battle and burnt out vehicles and tanks gave a real time feel for things that had taken place there recently. Vijay's Battalion had captured a Pakistani jeep in the earlier fighting near a Pak village named Jassaron, which we used to then tour the entire area of the conflict, visiting Attari, Khalra and Khemkaran sites one by one.

The captured and burnt out tanks at Patton-nagar, and the traces of the struggle that had been a close run thing in the Khemkaran Sector was still very fresh. Seeing is believing and this immediate effort at the personal level remained a vivid memory in my later years of service.

Finally we got to Hussainiwala near Ferozpur to see for ourselves how things had shaped there. A Maratha battalion had barely fended off a Pakistani attempt to capture the site of the great Indian patriot – Bhagat Singh's cremation. The British rulers had cremated him secretly at this site.

This self imposed effort and look around the fresh battle areas, gave me a great deal of self confidence in training and preparing for the future. I came away with a feeling that our handling of infantry in battle seemed unimaginative and some innovation of techniques to operate in battle should be worked out. I got back to 18 Rajput on the Sirhind Canal, and with the active encouragement of the CO, tried out some innovative ideas in the handling of infantry. These proved very useful later when I was commanding the Battalion in the War for the Liberation of Bangladesh. Large patches of sugar cane cultivation, short of the Sutlej River in the Machiwara area became our realistic and challenging training area. Zail Singh the Commanding Officer gave us the youngsters a lot of encouragement to keep at it. This period of bonding in the officers and Junior Commissioned Officers (JCOs) was to prove a great asset later in 1971.

During March 1966 I got posted back to the NEFA area as Brigade Major of a brigade in Sela, in the very midst of the area where in November 1962 Brigadier Hoshiar Singh's Brigade had failed dismally to put up any worthwhile fight and suffered ignomy and defeat. Here too I felt very disturbed that our infantry had been swamped with the Chinese literally massacring our men at will. Something was very wrong.

By spring of 1966 our Division had moved forward to re-occupy Sela. We were in the midst of the area that had been held by Brig Hoshiar's units. There were pathetic remnants of the setback we had suffered in November 1962. It was a touchy period for us as we were operating in an area where only a few years before we had been humiliated and defeated.

After a two year tenure with 77 Brigade, shortly after we were brought down to a lower altitude to Tenga, I had been moved back to 18 Rajput who were still licking their wounds after the clash with the Chinese at Nathula in Sikkim. The clash with the Chinese seemed a waste of precious lives as we had lost Major Harbhajan Singh and Subedar Raghav Prasad in the wire fence laying episode. Twenty other ranks were also killed in the pointless clash. It was the artillery which came down heavily on the Chinese to restore some order. Brigadier M M S Bakshi MVC, our Brigade Commander

had been in one of the bunkers at the sudden errupton of hostile Chinese fire and he narrated the events to me after I had joined. I had been in his syndicate during my Staff College Course. He had done conspicuously well with Hodson's Horse in the Sialkot Sector in the 1965 War with Pakistan.

I was already into my third consecutive year in the high altitude area in Sikkim, and the nomination for the Fort Benning course in USA came through seemingly in a timely manner. I reported at Army Headquarters and after all the preparations were complete, I was told at the very last moment that there was a hitch about my allowances. The course was cancelled at the very last moment since the Indian Finance Minister (Morarji Desai) refused the Army Headquater's suggestion to marginally increase the monetary allowance during the ten month sojourn in the USA. I got back to Sikkim and thus had another full years exposure at high altitude after the two years at Sela.

By end of 1968 we were moved down to Nasirabad in Rajasthan. Luck seemed to hold and the Fort Benning Course was revived for me and I set off in mid-January 1969 for the USA. This time accompanied by Usha, Kunal and Teesta who were provided the air tickets for the to and fro journey by a generous Mr. Nirmal Hoon, Usha's elder brother. I was permitted to take my family at my own expense.

*****

At Benning all my American classmates were Vietnam veterans. Most of their experience was in platoon and company level hard fought battles in the jungle and paddy field type terrain in Viet Nam. However, in the Advance Course most of the training exercises were confined to mechanized infantry operating in fast moving armour based operations in the European environment. I found it very absorbing learning how the mix of armour, mechanized infantry and engineers was to be handled. The very quick responses and control measures employed in such battle,

were heady new stuff for me. Use of helicopters, offensive air support and preponderous use of artillery and naval gun support was all very interesting things to learn about. I did well enough on the course and was given a 'Distinguished Allied Graduates' Trophy and Certificate at the termination.

At the end of our stay at Fort Benning as the nominated senior foreign officer amongst my batchmates, it fell to my lot to say a few words of thanks to the faculty members and classmates and their wives at the glittering farewell function.

We were back in Nasirabad for a few months before the Commandant at the Infantry School, had me posted as the Senior Instructor in charge of the Junior Commissioned Officers (JCOs) and Non Commissioned Officers (NCOs) training wing. I had a team of officers and JCO instructors who joined me in making the PC Course (as it was called) as interesting and exciting as could be.

Barely six months later orders were received for me to move back to Nasirabad to take command of 18 Rajput who were already preparing to move east again. This time to Mizoram insurgency area. It seemed odd that this unit had barely a year and a half of a peace station tenure and seemed logical that we would go westwards. It was too late to do anything about this as the Battalion was to move to the east in the first week of January 1971.

Command of an infantry battalion is crowning event in an infantry officer's career. I was just 35 years old at the time and putting on the coveted rank of a lieutenant colonel's rank felt nice (command of infantry units has since changed to Full Colonel's rank). We moved by military special along the metre gauge line. Usha and the children went back to Dehradun.

We were almost a week on the military special train. Making our way through Uttar Pradesh, Bihar, West Bengal into Assam. The Bramaputra bridge at Gauhati had come up by early 1971, so we carried on through Halflong to go to Masimpur. Instead of the whole unit going into the Mizoram district we were unexpectedly diverted to Agartala in Tripura. We offloaded at the railhead of

Dharmpur- which had us moving by hired transport to a place short of Agartala. The Battalion was poorly off for transport, radio equipment and even manpower. Some strength had been diverted to Virangte Jungle Warfare School at the entrance of the road leading to Aizwal in the Mizoram area.

Within a fortnight of our arrival in Tripura the events that finally led to the War of Bangladesh Liberation began to unfold. We got to witness the events that began with the hijacking of an Indian Airlines civilian plane and its destruction at Lahore in West Pakistan.

18 Rajput played a prominent part in the War and got the Battle Honour of 'Akhaura' and had a most dramatic role in the Battle of Ashuganj where the Pakistani 14 Divisional Commander, Major General Qazi Abdul Majid Khan had the giant Meghna Bridge blown during the Ashuganj battle, which led to General Sagat mounting a heliborne bypass operation that led to the dash to Dhaka and the stunning victory in the War.

A great deal of credit for suggesting and demonstrating the stratagem for the Akhaura battle was owed to 18 Rajput under my command successfully carrying out a preliminary operation at Mukandpur on 19 November 1971.

The significance of the preliminary Mukandpur operation, should be viewed in perspective after the very messy conduct of the Dhalai Battle at the end of October 1971 under the overall control of Lt Gen Sagat Singh himself, with our GOC Major General B F Gonsalves and 61 Brigade's three infantry battalions and almost the full artillery brigade's support. This Dhalai operation was in support of a East Bengal Battalion. Brigadier S D Yadav, the Brigade Commander and Lt Col Devasan CO of 7 Raj Rif were badly injured. Ultimately Pak 30 Frontier Force under a valiant Major Javed fought tooth and nail. Ultimately Brigadier K P Pandey (Tom) ultimately took matters in hand and with the use of skilled artillery fire overcame the opposition. Pak Maj Javed was killed and his troops suffered 160 killed and injured in the battle.

Brigadier Mishra (my brigade commander) had acknowledged that the divisional battle for Akhaura was fought almost exactly on the pattern of the 'Mukandpur' affair.

My own motivation of ensuring that the memory of the disgraceful performance of 1962 was wiped out and we came out the clear winners in this, drove me and my unit to do well at all cost. I felt firmly that the use of the stratagem by a combined use of stealth and firepower, would minimize casualties and bring us success. Mukandpur action had proved this beyond any doubt.

* * * * *

After the de-induction from Dhaka in March 1972, the Battalion was in Agartala for almost a year after which it was inducted into eastern Mizoram in the counter-insurgency role. I was selected for the coveted Higher Command Course on completion of my tenure of three years of command. The Battalion was in the Mizoram district by the time I left them. I was thus the first officer from the Rajput Regiment to be given this exposure. The Higher Command Course had been instituted at the College of Combat at Mhow to expose selected officers for higher command in their later career.

* * * * *

At the end of the year long Higher Command course, I was posted to the Staff College as an instructor or Directing Staff. This was a much sought after prize posting where after a three year tenure I was next posted to New Delhi as a staff officer in the Military Wing of the Cabinet Secretariat. I was secretary to the Chief's of Staff Committee (COSC), a sensitive exposure.

THE TSO-KAR SNOW-LEOPARD
(PANTHERA UNCIAL SCHREBER)

By mid 1980, I had been posted to command an infantry brigade in eastern Ladakh. This was again a posting in high altitude area. This was my fourth tenure in such hard area. It came about when Harjit Talwar, a gunner coursemate declined this appointment owing to some hearing (ear) problem. I was to take over a brigade in the Akhnur Sector but found myself catapulted into Ladakh at short notice. 70 Brigade had a nasty reputation of having had several previous brigadiers falling out owing to health problems, brought on by sustained exposure to harsh conditions. This was well accepted fact was known and accepted in the Military Secretary's Branch – but given a go by in my case.

Not given to making too much of a fuss about such issues, I readily took up the appointment in early May 1980. After acclimatizing as required, I moved to Kiari where my brigade Headquarters was located astride the Indus River in a narrow valley.

Ladakh is easily the hardest of the high altitude areas to serve in. Being a high altitude desert area with very scant rain or snow, it has hardly any vegetation to sustain life. Few local villages had cheerful Ladakhis clinging to small holdings next to the few snowfed streams cascading down narrow rocky nalas. It is

THE TSO-KAR SNOW-LEOPARD

a land of wide spaces and has wildlife unique to such altitude and conditions. The birdlife too has adapted to these conditions. For me, with my sharp eyes for wildlife, it was a land of heightened perceptions.

As one drove to Kiari along the tarmac road carved out by the Border Road efforts, I would keep craning my neck to lookout for *bharals* (blue sheep *Pseudois nayaur*), and *shapus* (Urial *Ovis orientalis*) that seemed to somehow find precarious foothold in the sheer towering rock faces that rose sharply on both sides of the Indus. Large flocks of *turkoman rock pigeons*, with their distinctive white band across their tail fans, would scatter in flight as we drove on. Invariably, a few *chakor* (a mountain partridge) would be sighted in the narrow strips of land besides the road at places. I had given up all shooting whilst in Ladakh and found it helpful that I could keep my interest in these matters alive.

From Tibet the Indus River entered my sector near Demchok and flowed uninterrupted between the Chinese controlled Kailash Range on its northern side and the Zanskar Range on its southern side. It's a wide open glacier valley upto the Loma Bend, after which the valley narrows down after flowing past Nyoma. Thereafter it enters an extended narrow gorge that only opens up near Karu before flowing on towards Leh. The Sector was roughly 300 kilometres wide and of similar depth. My HQ at Kiari was located midway in the narrow gorge. The sound of the flowing river remained omnipresent until the onset of winter when we suddenly woke up in a silent valley as the river had frozen over.

From a post called Tsakala one could look into the flanking sector's Chushul area and we could get a clear view of the Rezangla feature on which a company of 13 Kumaon under Major Shaitan Singh had heroically held on against overwhelming Chinese attacks during November 1962.

*****

The Puga Valley

From Kiari if you directly climb southwards, after a stiff and steep climb of about two thousand feet you emerge onto the Kimne Plateau. The plateau slopes away further southwards into a vast salt lake called Tso Kar. A small collection of stone huts of local graziers looking like a smudgy dark blur when viewed from a helicopter, had the local village name of Pogu Nagu.

THE TSO-KAR SNOW-LEOPARD

This graziers village was used by the pashmina goatherds as a forward base for staging through their large flocks of these goats as winter approached each year. This requires some explaining and understanding.

Ladakh gets very little or no snow even in winter. To conserve the sparse growth of grass in the lower valleys, the Ladakhi graziers push their large flocks of pashmina goats onto the higher reaches to thereafter move down as the sparse snow fall occurs with intensification of winter. The Pongu Nagu staging village helps them to do this in the area between Tso Kar lake and Taglang La pass through which the road from Rohtang Pass (near Manali), leads you to Upshi and then Leh. This vast area of a jumble of rocky high ground looks barren to us but the locals use every blade of grass that grows there as food for their flocks of pashmina goats. This is an annual feature and you only find the large flocks of the goats near the scant villages next to the Indus only later in the passing phase of the winter. Any unusual change in the pattern of snowfall can seriously disrupt this delicately balanced arrangement.

On my returning from leave in December of 1980, I learnt of a sudden crisis having developed owing to unusually heavy and early snowfall in the Tso Kar and surrounding heights. All the large flocks of goats with their goatherds were trapped on the heights and were starving for want of fodder in the snow covered environment. Mr. Phunsok, the District Commissioner requested Major General KK Sudan to help out with fodder, kerosine for fuel and some rations. This was promptly organised by Colonel Naveen Maini who was officiating in my place. A convoy of three-ton vehicles carried the stuff required, using the little used track via Mahe, the Puga Valley and over the Polokang Kala Pass to Pongu Nagu. This timely aid to the local population was highly appreciated by the civilian government and local population.

But there was a catch in the situation. The convoy of diesel vehicles all ran out of fuel on the return trip. Owing to the altitude

the snowfall was powdery and leading to excessive use of fuel due to lack of traction in the powdery snow. In some panic but in an organized manner the vehicles were allowed to freeze over and the drivers and men walked back to safety. On arrival back from leave I found this very disturbing and carried out a helicopter trip to assess matters and did not like the look of things. You never abandon your dead in battle or your equipment like precious vehicles in such a heartless manner.

A full scale operation had to be organized to lay a telephone line as a rescue team made their way to the stranded vehicles, heated the transmission systems and extricated the vehicles one by one. It took time and was hard work but was done in a satisfactory manner. The cold was so intense that year that even the kerosine oil froze in the jerricans.

Tso Morari Lake

On the last day of the operation of rescuing the stranded vehicles I along with a couple of supporting fleet of Jonga jeeps drove over the same route to Pongu Nagu. As we crossed the Polokang Kala Pass we came across a large flock of *Ram Chakor (Snowcock)*. They seemed to be in some haste to get away in the snow uphill of us as we passed. They are big ungainly birds but climb the hill in a steady measured manner. Further on as we got closer to Pongu Nagu, I saw a dead yak lying in the snow about seventy five yards off the track with some Himalayan ravens feeding on the carrion. Without giving it much thought we drove on in the blinding whiteness around us. I was driving using the large snow goggles to minimize the all prevailing glare.

After an hour or so we started back and this time I saw an animal leaving the dead yak lying in the snow. The dead yak's black and stark red flesh against the white background lay about seventy yards away from the road. This time in the blurred whiteness I saw an animal leave the yak carcase and hurry across our front. I initially thought it was one of those large mastiff Ladakhi dogs but realized suddenly that the long bushy tail behind him could only be that of a snow leopard. The animal disappeared into the white fastness of the "white out" conditions. The glare was quite blinding. I stopped the Jonga jeep at the place where the animal had run across but the slush and melting snow made the pugmark impossible to read.

I had mentioned this unusual sighting of the very elusive animal in the Tso Kar area to General Rodrigues, who had replaced Sudan as the General Officer Commanding of the Leh Division, of which my brigade was a part. Film-makers the Bedi Brothers shot a film on the snow leopard in the adjacent area near the Tso Morari lake next to the *Kharzuk* Gompa. Tso Morari lake is the breeding area for the *Bar Headed Geese* that arrive there in spring every year. The parent birds nest in the rocks on the slopes above the lake and shed their pinion feathers when they have laid their eggs. They grow back their flying wings with their chicks doing so with them. They fly away together in early winter.

* * * * *

TIGER IN THE TRIANGLE

Being a bit of a "Jungle Salt", I got drawn into a concerted attempt of getting young officer leadership of the Army in particular and the Armed forces in general, in the effort of protecting and preserving wildlife countryside. Lt Gen Sunderjee as the General Officer Commander-in- Chief of Western Command, was assisted in this by Maj Gen Ramu Gaur, the then Area Commander covering Punjab, Haryana and Himachal. Gen Gaur suggested my name for the task. We had a fruitful time during my earlier Ladakh tenure. He was completely hooked to photography and he found my wildlife interest and knowledge of some help. He had been Gen Rodrigue's Deputy at Leh.

I was asked to organize a fortnights' programme for young officers of Western Command units at the Bharatpur Bird and Sariska Wildlife Sanctuaries. The effort was of exposing young officers to the thrill and knowledge of the Jungle. It aimed at arousing interest in birds and fauna of the Indian jungle of our vast country. With the help of film and slide shows followed by talks and some lectures by eminent naturalists. It created a 'Wave' of awareness that the Army could help in the protection of this valuable national asset. Hitherto the Army has been generally accused of irresponsible and wanton destruction of wildlife.

We were greatly assisted by the Bombay Natural History Society, and the Sanctuary Magazine publishers. The Rajasthan Forest Department was also most cooperative and helpful.

Though initially confined to the Western Command, this programme emphasised that in all the border areas, including the high Himalayas and the dense jungles of the Northeast, the infinite variety of wildlife needs to be studied in greater detail and not just be taken for granted. The role played by the Territorial Army Ecological units in their restorative work also needed to be understood and appreciated. The Wild life Institute being set up in Dehradun, had a important role in developing this awareness and culture.

In later years this effort of involving the Army in the protection of wildlife took a more formal shape. Gen Sunderji followed this up when he became the Chief.

*****

Barely after a year in New Delhi in a staff job, I was posted in to Jammu to command the prestigious 26 Infantry Division in November 1986. For me It meant that I had done a full circuit from those early days in mid 1956 when I had joined at Samba in the same area as a young subaltern. Much had changed in the interim period.

The gallery of 'rogues' in the GOC's office had photographs ranging from Sam Maneckshaw to Kumaramangalam and Krishna Rao. The 'Tiger in the Trangle' formation sign indicated that the Division had been raised during the World War in the Bengal delta region. It had performed very creditably under Maj Gen Lomax in the Arakan operations. My erstwhile battalion, 2nd Battalion, had earned a hard fought Battle-Honour –'Point 551' against the Japanese in the Buthidang area of the Arakans during World War ii in May 1944..

After joining at Jammu, I at times had a vague memory of having travelled by train from Lahore and Sialkot in 1942. I had been just a seven year old with my parents for our very memorable holiday in the valley. Now as the commander of the Division, I could view from a helicopter the old railway alignment from Sialkot which had the refugees settled along it after the disused line was uprooted.

At the Baloul Golf Course at Miran Sahib a solitary signal semifore stood isolated on a bund, its rusted signal arm frozen in irony of the troubled times after partitition. A painted sign declared that a bottle of Scoth Whiskey would be awarded to any golfer hitting the arm of the signal with the ball during play.

* * * * *

Picture of self as Col of Rajput Regt

It was at Jammu that I got word that I had been elected the Sixth Colonel of The Rajput Regiment by a system of voting that enabled all the officers who had ten years service or more to exercise their choice. This was a great honour and opportunity for me. I now had the mandate to change the culture and image of the Regimental Centre at Fatehgarh in central UP. How this was achieved, is a story by itself, For me and my family members, this became the crowning achievement of a lifetime of dedicated soldiering.

Fatehgarh — The Rajput Regiment War Memorial — 1991

EPILOGUE

These stories have been written in an endeavour to preserve the memory of an eventful life over the last 70 years or so. It is not meant to look mournfully into the past, but to remember it to have been a thrilling and eventful and joyous life. It is however in no way meant to be a boastful record of the past.

In the Army, particularly in the infantry, it was the logical way of life which thrived on the attributes of a "Jungle Salt" and sharpened ones perceptions and reflexes in the use of ground and weapons. It certainly helped develop a quickness of the eye and responses to overcome unexpected and tight situations.

The great English Nobel Laureate Sir Bertrand Russel in his book – "How to Achieve Happiness" has commented on the subject of hunting, as being one of man's oldest and most deeply satisfying hobbies – and that the instinct is present in most men in a dormant state.

This instinct maybe indulged in now with a difference – changing the killing part to photographing instead.

Exchange the rifle for a camera.

SOME THOUGHTS

The last couple of years of our son Kunal's schooling coincided with my being posted to the Defence Services Staff College in Wellington, Nilgiris. The Doon School, among all its other pluses, actively encouraged an outdoor bent of mind. During the school vacations, most of the weekends at Wellington were spent fishing for rainbow trout in the upper reaches of the Blue Mountains. The sheer beauty of the surroundings provided the opportunity to build on his already growing interest in nature. In the mid-1970s, labels like 'naturalists' and 'conservationists' did not exit, and in a way he had to cut out his own path.

By the time Kunal graduated from college, subconsciously he had more or less decided on what he wanted to do. The first opportunity he got, he signed up with 'Tiger Tops', a British owned adventure tourism company. His job profile required him to primarily help a subsidiary company, 'Mountain Travel India', reccee and open up trekking routes between the Kashmir Valley and Zanskar; Zanskar and Ladakh; and also Ladakh and the Nubra region. During the winter months, with temperatures in Ladakh plummeting into the minus zone, the entire team shifted to Nepal, again training in white water running and working as 'Naturalists' at the Tiger Tops Lodge in the Royal Chitwan National Park. Barely in his 20s, this would prove to be excellent training ground for some of the films and books that he produced subsequently. *'The Long Road to Siachen: The Question Why'* published by Rupa &

Co. in 2011 draws heavily on his ground experience of the Trans-Himalayan region.

Post Tiger Tops, he joined India Today for a brief period, before moving on to the Associated Press. Here his focus was on environmental issues, a area that was still quite a blank on the mental make up of the country at the time. During this period his work brought him into contact with some of the icons of Indian Wildlife and despite their age difference, soon became close friends; HS Panwar, the then Director of Project Tiger, S Deb Roy and Pranabes Sanyal, the Field Directors of the Manas and Sunderbans Tiger Reserves, and a host of others.

During this period, the Army was beginning to take its first nascent steps towards an environmental awakening. The Chief of Army Staff, General K Sundarji tasked me to conduct a wildlife preservation workshop. This was held at Bharatpur and the Sariska Tiger Reserve over a few days. One of the reasons for its path breaking success was the rapport that already existed between Kunal and the wildlife authorities. This was just the beginning, for this was soon followed by a second workshop in Dachigam that was held under the guidance of Lt Gen RK Gaur, who himself was a superb photographer and naturalist. The third workshop conducted by Eastern Command involved my brother Vijay, who was posted in Calcutta at the time. This movement over the years has had an extremely positive impact on areas that are under the Army's control. Most importantly, it helped in curtailing the wanton slaughter of wildlife that some army units were guilty of in those days.

Some critical issues Kunal focused on during that period involved Rhino poaching in Kaziranga (he even got nicked in the foot after getting into a firefight with poachers); the ivory trade and the slaughter of elephants by electrocution in South India; the man-eating problem in the Sunderbans; and the outbreak of child lifting by wolves in the Hazaribagh region among others.

His close circle of friends at the time included Royina Grewal, the Delhi correspondent of Sanctuary Magazine. Through Royina, in January 1986, Bittu Sahgal asked Kunal to get involved with his 16-part Project Tiger television series. With no experience of film making, his involvement being subject specific, Kunal moved from the world of wire service journalism to an environment where at the time everything was being shot on 16mm. Video was virtually non-existent and after a fair amount of coaxing, Bittu managed to cobble together a shooting crew, put it under the directional control of Kunal and sent them off to Sariska Tiger Reserve.

Cameramen, in this case Film Institute graduates, were far more comfortable shooting under controlled conditions where their work was simply superb. Wildlife filming in India, unlike the open savannas of Africa, was an extremely challenging business where one had to spend hours looking for an animal who when located would barely give the camera a second take. In relative terms, Sariska was one of the easier reserves to shoot. Yet, towards the end of the first film, there had been enough problems to have Bittu Sahgal contemplate asking Kunal to take on the task of cinematography as well.

Brijender Singh who was a close confidante of Prime Minister Rajiv Gandhi and a Honorary Wildlife Warden was filming Corbett; Romulus Whitaker and Shekhar Dattatri together were working on Periyar while Tejbir Singh and Valmik Thapar were falling back on their large bank of tiger footage to tell the tale of Ranthambhore. Melghat, Nagarjuna Saagar and the Bandipur films were eventually shot by other mixed crews. Literally learning on the job in the Sunderbans – Bittu Sahgal's hand was forced as the cameraman pulled out while the crew was headed for the airport - Kunal was to go on to shoot and make the films on Pallamau (Bihar), Buxa (North Bengal), Manas (Assam), Namdapha (Arunachal), Simlipal (Orissa), Indravati and Kanha (both in Madhya Pradesh). In addition, while shooting for Sanctuary Films, he also shot the wildlife sections for the Rakshak serial in Kashmir and Ladakh.

The Project Tiger series of films – edited and given final direction by Dipti Bhalla, had a major impact on the Indian public's awareness of our wildlife reserves. The films were aired by Doordarshan, the only television channel at the time immediately on the tail of the blockbuster series – "the Ramayan" – every Sunday morning.

I have little doubt in my mind that Project Tiger has been one of the most successful conservation projects in the subcontinent. Apart from bringing the focus on to the plight of the tiger, the project also did yeoman service to the nation by identifying diversely different eco-systems for protection. Project Tiger not only impacted the surviving tiger populations, but also had a role to play in the conservation of many species. Today, Project Tiger has under its ambit some fifty-odd sanctuaries and National Parks and its role has changed somewhat from its initial days. While the situation in many parts of the country continue to be fairly grim, at least Project Tiger provided a peg on which conservationists could hang their hat on and gear up for some sort of a fight.

One important lesson emerged extremely strongly from the wildlife workshops that we had conducted in the mid-1980s. If the Army could be involved in conservation projects, things could be done and seemingly hopeless scenarios be reversed. A case in point was the creation of the Army Eco-task Force that was given the task of reclaiming the Mussooriee Hills. Lime stone quarries, over the years, had ravaged the Himalayan foothills. Despite Dehradun being the home of the Forest Research Institute at the time, it was left to the local people, the judiciary and the Army to reclaim the area.

One such suggestion that could merit a thought would be to tap the large body of ex-Servicemen and create one or more Eco-battalion *in each and every state of India*. These units can be jointly officered by former Army officers and conservationists who are trained for the job. This force could be under the Ministry of Forest and Wildlife, having a dual operative system akin to the structure of the Assam Rifles which is under the Home Ministry but officered by the Indian Army. This concept, if developed and taken further, can change the very face of our country over the next couple of decades.

The Project Tiger television series created an awareness of our natural resources amongst our people in a big way, sometimes even creating a bit too much human interest that was detrimental to the eco-system. Nevertheless, as a natural progression, Kunal along with Dipti then formed KaleidoIndia which went on to shoot the *Call of the Wild* series of films for the Department of Tourism. This series had divided the subcontinent into five zones; Western India covered Gir, the Desert National Park, Ranthambhore and Sariska; South India focused on Kabini (Nagarhole), Bandipur, the Nilgiris and Periyar; Central India looked at Kanha, Bandavgarh and Pallamau; Eastern India covered the Sunderbans, Kaziranga and Namdapha; and Northern India took in its sweep the Hemis National Park (Ladakh), Corbett and Dudhwa.

*****

Teesta our second child has contributed some telling photographs of wildlife. Both the cover and back photographs were taken at Kanha in 1995.

Teesta works for the travel trade and is based in Delhi.

*****

Ashok and Usha Verma reside at Windsong Cottage, Bandrol beyond Kullu. They spend most of their time growing some flowers in their hill home.

*****

ABOUT THE AUTHOR

Major General Ashok Kalyan Verma, the author of *"Jungle Odyssey – A Soldier's Memoirs"*, has been a prominent figure in The Rajput Regiment. Many years my elder, he has been a role model and noticeable officer in almost every rank he has held from his early years. Both he and his younger brother, Colonel Vijay, served in several Battalions of the Regiment and were both greatly admired by the rank and file, and were well known for their wider interest in Wildlife and Shikar.

One of the Limhaipur Tigers that Captain Ashok Verma had shot in January 1960, is still preserved as a much valued trophy in the 2nd Battalion Officer's Mess. Similarly, a 'Maharana Pratap' carved from the ivory of the tusker shot at Barkot, reminds successive generation of Officers of 13 Mechanised Infantry (earlier 18th Battalion of The Rajput Regiment) of the spectacular role played by the Unit in the **War** for the Liberation of Bangladesh in 1971. Lieutenant Colonel Ashok Verma was the Commanding Officer in that War, during which his Battalion was awarded the Battle Honour of AKHAURA. 18 Rajput had fought a major battle at ASHUGANJ on the Meghna Bridge on 9th December and had entered Dhaka on 16 December afternoon as a part of Lieutenant General Sagat Singh's 4 Corps.

In keeping with the value systems and trends in the early years after Indian Independence, the Army was at that time a much sought after profession. It was not just an occupation but a way of life. Like much of those who joined the Services in the Fifties, the officer material came from similar background and in many cases from families of officers who had served in other government civil services during the Raj. "Jungle Odyssey" glimpses some of the prevalent trends of those times. The Verma brothers were the sons of Mr Narendra Singh Verma, one such officer of the Civil Service of the then Central Province (CP). A little later as an officer of the Indian Administrative Service (IAS) he played

ABOUT THE AUTHOR

a prominent part in the District level administration in several districts after the Hyderabad Police Action of September 1948. These included Adilabad, Nanded and Nizamabad. Mr N S Verma was later Custodian of Evacuee Property in Hyderabad and then Regional Settlement Commissioner for South and Western India, based in Mumbai for several years. Mr Verma was known for his unimpeachable integrity.

Hyderabad later became the state capital of Andhra. Much of the area in which the events narrated took place have been incorporated in the state of Maharashtra later.

Major General Ashok Verma was elected the Colonel of The Rajput Regiment in 1986 by a popular vote. He was the Sixth Colonel of the Regiment after Field Marshal K M Cariappa OBE. It is to his credit that Fatehgarh, the Home of the Regiment, got a facelift that has turned it into an impressive Infantry Regimental Centre.

His personal character and professional handling of the large Infantry Regiment, that comprises the many Battalions, created a noticeable wave of alround quality improvement. He had made special efforts to revive historical links with the older Units that have been part of the Regiment. These included the affiliation and links with Indian Naval Ships RAJPUT and RANA and 15 Squadron of the Indian Air Force. Similarly, 4 GUARDS (1 Rajput), 17 Para Fd (8 Rajput) and 23 Mech Inf (20 Rajput), and 5 Fd Regt.

After a distinguished career in the Army, on retirement, the General wrote several books, of which *"River's of Silence"* deals with the 1962 Operations against China and also describes 1971 operations in Bangladesh.

The book *"Blood on the Snow"* on Kargil Operations 1999, has been much acclaimed, as it is the only book amongst the Indian authors which deals with the operations at a Strategic level. The treatment of strategy during the operations, has been greatly appreciated by serious students of military history.

He again wrote *"Bridge on River Meghna"* on 1971 Operations in Bangladesh after having validated his research consequent to his re-visit to the areas where he had operated.

Despite laurels as an author in matters military, he did not feel content till put down on paper, his experiences as a youth under the benign guidance of his father who was a senior Administrator in Central Provinces.

One can literally smell the 'jungles' in this book, much like his idol the great Jim Corbett. General Verma has re-established his credentials as a writer, whose books are not only worth a read but a valuable reference to issues on Environment and its preservation.

General Ashok resides in a village beyond Kullu in Himachal, where his wife and he grow some flowers in a rock filled garden.

Both the brothers had become staunch conservationist of Wildlife when still in service.

Milan Naidu
Lt Gen (Retd) PVSM AVSM YSM
former Vice Chief of Army Staff and
Colonel of the Rajput Regiment,
presently Member of the Armed Forces Tribunal.